FROM
DRIFT
TO
DRIVE

FROM
DRIFT
TO
DRIVE

A HIGH ACHIEVER'S GUIDE
TO BREAKING THE CHAINS
OF COMPLACENCY

....

CHRIS ROBINSON

FOREWORD BY
JOHN C. MAXWELL

FROM DRIFT TO DRIVE:
A High Achiever's Guide to Breaking the Chains of Complacency

© 2025 Chris Robinson

All rights reserved. No part of this publication may be reproduced, stored in a retrieval system, or transmitted in any form by any means, electronic, mechanical, photocopy, recording, or otherwise, without the prior permission of the publisher, except as provided by USA copyright law.

No patent liability is assumed with respect to the use of the information contained herein. Although every precaution has been taken in the preparation of this book, the publisher and author assume no responsibility for errors or omissions. Neither is any liability assumed for damages resulting from the use of the information contained herein.

Scripture quotations marked KJV are taken from the King James Version. Public Domain.

Scripture quotations marked NIV are taken from the Holy Bible, New International Version®, NIV®. Copyright © 1973, 1978, 1984, 2011 by Biblica, Inc.® Used by permission of Zondervan. All rights reserved worldwide. www.zondervan.com. The "NIV" and "New International Version" are trademarks registered in the United States Patent and Trademark Office by Biblica, Inc.®

Published by Maxwell Leadership Publishing,
an imprint of Forefront Books.
Distributed by Simon & Schuster.

Library of Congress Control Number: 2025910279

Print ISBN: 9798887100500
E-book ISBN: 9798887100517

Cover Design by Studio Gearbox
Interior Design by Mary Susan Oleson, Blu Design Concepts

Printed in the United States of America
25 26 27 28 29 30 [RR4] 10 9 8 7 6 5 4 3 2 1

THIS BOOK IS DEDICATED TO the thousands of Maxwell Leadership Certified Team Members around the world, especially those who have been with the Team since the beginning. It is both an honor and a privilege to be a part of your journey and I am grateful to have you as a part of mine.

Contents

Foreword by John C. Maxwell 9

SECTION ONE: *Asleep at the Wheel* 13

Rumble Strips *15*

Where Complacency Hides *29*

SECTION TWO: *The Seven Step Framework* 45

Step 1: Clarity: You Cannot Have What You Cannot See *47*

Step 2: Gathering: Learn a Little, Do a Little *69*

Step 3: Filtering: How to Find the Gold *87*

Step 4: Guidance: The Bridge to Experience and Wisdom *111*

Step 5: Relationships: The Right Rooms *129*

Step 6: Action: One Mile at a Time *149*

Step 7: Evaluating: Four Questions That Keep You on Target ... *169*

SECTION THREE: *Back in the Driver's Seat* .. 191

When Reality Meets the Road *193*

Acknowledgments *207*

Notes *209*

FOREWORD

BY *John C. Maxwell*

....

There are two kinds of people in the world: those who drift through life and those who take ownership of their journey.

The difference isn't talent, intelligence, or luck. It's a decision. A decision to take action, to grow, and to refuse to let complacency have the final say. That's what this book is about. And there's no one better to guide you through it than my friend Chris Robinson.

Long before he was the executive vice president of Maxwell Leadership, Chris was one of the first members of the Maxwell Leadership Certified Team. From the very beginning, he stood out—not just because of his passion for leadership, but because of his ability to help people move forward.

Chris and I are more than colleagues—we're great friends. Over the years, I've had a front-row seat to his journey, watching him go from a hungry student of leadership to a world-class coach, speaker, and mentor. And through it all, I've seen one defining characteristic in him: He refuses to let complacency win.

Maybe you've reached a level of success, but you feel stuck. Maybe you have a dream, but you've been waiting for the *perfect*

FOREWORD

moment to pursue it. Or maybe you're simply going through the motions, unsure of how to move forward. If any of that sounds familiar, this book is for you.

Chris lays out a proven road map—the Seven Step Framework—that will help you break free from drift and create the momentum you need to move forward. This isn't about hype. It's not about working harder or "hustling" your way to success. It's about being intentional—taking focused, strategic action that leads to real, lasting results.

One of the things I love most about Chris is that he's not just a teacher—he's a practitioner. He's walked this journey himself, and he knows what it takes to push past obstacles, silence doubt, and keep growing.

So, here's my challenge to you: Don't just read this book. Apply it. Take the steps Chris lays out. Do the work. And watch what happens when you commit to your own growth. I believe in you. And I believe in the power of what Chris has written in these pages.

Your friend,
John C. Maxwell

SECTION ONE:

ASLEEP
AT THE
WHEEL

Rumble Strips

I politely thanked him, took the smooth white envelope from his hand, and closed the door.

In some ways, it felt like my life was over.

The sheriff had shown up on my doorstep with the news and the paperwork that our home—the house my wife and I had built, the place for which we'd meticulously chosen the tile and the paint colors and the furnishings—was no longer ours. That envelope held the legal documents finalizing the foreclosure on our dream home. The dual barrels of a recent career change and a real estate market turned upside down came blasting through the peaceful domestic life we'd carefully created. All the work, heart, and dreams that went into the life we were leading collapsed in a less-than-subtle cymbal crash.

Did I mention that my wife, Jenee, had just given birth to our triplets at the time?

Oh yeah. There was that too...um, three.

I turned and looked out the arched bank of two-story windows that framed our backyard, a thicket of tall trees just beyond the fence line. That backyard where my babies, once they were toddlers, were supposed to play. Those trees I gazed at each morning over my first cup of coffee and watched the sun set behind each evening. The flower bed of little shrubs we wouldn't ever see spread and grow.

This life, the one I thought was going to be lived out in this house, was done.

However, when that sheriff handed over that news and that envelope, I was also being handed a gift. Something beyond what I could currently see. Something bigger.

I thought I had arrived at the ceiling of my success in that tidy atrium ranch house in that tidy suburb of St. Louis. I was comfortable with what I had achieved.

Instead, I was only beginning. This moment would be the thing that would pull me out of the complacency I'd allowed to creep into my life. It would make me grab the wheel of where I wanted to go with more focus, instead of letting things casually drift to the shoulder. It would wake me up to a world of possibilities instead of letting me continue to slumber in my self-satisfaction. It would lead me to where I am today.

It was a gift, alright. Minus the sheriff and the foreclosure (hopefully), it's the very same gift now in front of you.

Good Enough

When I started talking about my heartbeat for this book with my team, at first I thought about something I could share with the people I encounter who seem to be struggling to find their way, bouncing

RUMBLE STRIPS

from thing to thing, never quite getting into their groove. But as the conversations and the ideas began to grow, I realized something. This book wasn't for that person.

This book is for *you*. The achiever. The builder. The visionary.

You've done some things in your day. You've conquered mountains, climbed ladders, and accomplished an impressive list of accolades.

Now what?

You see, in working with leaders and coaches across the globe, high-capacity people who have achieved amazing things in their lives, I've seen something. There's a smoke, if you will, that winds its way into those places and spaces where we've hit a certain level of achievement and satisfaction. It's so subtle we often don't even realize it's there, circled around our ankles, stealing oxygen from the room. It attempts to smother out the fires in our hearts, the drive and passion we used to have for goals and dreams. The haze it brings obscures our vision and reduces the wind in our sails. We sit in the calm waters, often thinking we've arrived somewhere instead of realizing we're adrift in a sea of complacency.

Yes, complacency. *Complacency* is a funny word because, on the one hand, it can mean that you're comfortable, that things have paid off to a certain extent and you're good with the results. But complacency has a darker side, a secret set of fangs that can be all too easy for an accomplished person like yourself to miss.

Seeing the phenomenon over and over again, seeing powerhouse people shifting into neutral, feeling myself sometimes living that way, has led me into an absolute fascination with the problem of complacency. I've scoured the history books to see where it's shown

FROM DRIFT TO DRIVE

up in any number of landmark events. I've pondered the plight of top government leaders and athletes and celebrities who finish out their careers with a mumble instead of a bang. What happened? How can uncommon accomplishments lead to such a boring yawn?

Consider the following examples of complacency:

Pax Romana in Pieces: The Roman Empire was unlike anything society had ever seen. Based on the ideals of operating as a republic, Rome dominated the world for over five hundred years in economic, military, and territorial power. However you look at the achievements of Rome, make no mistake: Those who were top achievers in Rome enjoyed wealth, comfort, and success. There were issues in Rome, to be sure. Unrest, struggle, ethical hypocrisies. But so many of those inconvenient truths seemed far away to those who had reached a certain level of status and influence.

Until it all fell down.

Historians today say that the Roman Empire collapsed due in large part to complacency.[1] An intentional ignoring of the change that was coming. An assumption that things would continue to work as they had. A negligence of the need to continue to innovate, evaluate, and navigate. The leaders of the empire failed to see the changes in the world because they thought they *were* the world.

RUMBLE STRIPS

43: Richard Petty is one of the most accomplished NASCAR drivers in the history of the sport, known by his race car's iconic number 43. He retired in 1992, after racing for thirty-four years. He won at Daytona seven times. During the course of his career, he racked up all kinds of records and wins, earning him the nickname "The King." But in the last eight years of his career, something happened.

He just stopped winning.

How could someone who had defined the sport simply lag behind?

Richard Petty himself explained it. As cars with better technologies—with superior tires and systems—entered the track, he made a choice for complacency. He said, "We'd been winning for twenty years and decided we wouldn't change. We should have led the way [in technology], but we didn't even follow."[2]

His honest insight into what happened reminds me of this quote from Bill Gates: "Success is a lousy teacher. It seduces smart people into thinking they can't lose."[3]

The List: Kmart. Blockbuster. Pan Am. Circuit City. Kodak. Radio Shack. TWA. Zenith.

Enough said.

FROM DRIFT TO DRIVE

* * * * *

I define complacency as *that secret place of satisfactory success*.

You may be looking at my definition of complacency and thinking, *Whoa, Chris. What's so wrong with that?*

Exactly.

That's your first indicator that complacency has crept into your life, when you've unconsciously slipped into the idea that where you are is good enough.

But *is* it good enough?

Really?

And what about the dangers of complacency?

Dangers, Chris?

Really? Isn't that a bit overstated?

Not from where I sit. Listen, the world in which we live seemingly changes overnight. Businesses that were "too big to fail" yesterday are vaporized in today's industry climate.

In doing research for this book, I came across a phrase that I just can't get out of my head. Are you ready for it?

Victory Disease.

Come on. That's an amazing way to describe the complacency you and I face.

It's a military description of what happens when a series of battlefield successes leads to complacency on the part of a nation or a leader. Historians say it originated with a Japanese concept, 戦勝病, or *senshoubyou*. It describes what happens when a series of victories leads to a lack of focus and a kind of arrogance that success is always assured.[4]

RUMBLE STRIPS

One example of Victory Disease is the attack on Pearl Harbor (a success in the eyes of the Japanese military) and the subsequent catastrophe for the Japanese at the Battle of Midway. The attack on Pearl Harbor in December of 1941 resulted in nineteen US ships being sunk or severely damaged and 2,403 people being killed. Japan went on to win several other decisive skirmishes in the Southeast Asia area of the Pacific. Six months later, in June of 1942, Admiral Matome Ugakiwas, the architect and leader of these attacks, was ready to launch another surprise attack on the United States, utilizing many of the same techniques and approaches from previous victories.

It didn't occur to him that American code breakers had intercepted their communications and were well aware of his plans.[5]

His Victory Disease cost the Japanese navy all of its aircraft carriers and its top pilots as the American military turned the tables on the Japanese forces and instead brought a surprise attack to them. The Battle of Midway, the result of that sneak attack, is considered pivotal to the outcome of World War II.[6]

Admiral Ugakiwas isn't alone. Historians point to Napoleon and his failed march on Russia. Victory Disease is also what I see when I look at what happened to the space shuttle *Challenger*; previous successful missions made top decision-makers complacent about important safety thresholds. I see shades of it in the Enron collapse, and in brands and businesses that soared to heights and then folded a few years later.

There's a verse in the Old Testament of the Bible that I keep coming back to. It's found in the book of Proverbs, an incredible collection of wisdom from teachers, kings, and leaders spanning almost three hundred years, from about 970 until 697 BC. This particular proverb comes from a king named Solomon, considered by several faiths to be the wisest man of his time. Proverbs 1:32 says, "The complacency of fools will destroy them" (NIV).

I dug in a little deeper, looking at the original language to see what kind of complacency wise old Solomon was talking about. What I found hit me right between the eyes.

The word for *complacency* in the original means *careless security.*[7] Just take a minute. Let that sink in. Where are you and I getting careless, due to what we've already achieved?

Where are we getting nonchalant? With our marriage relationship? With our spiritual journey? With our integrity? With our health?

Careless security turns out to be no guarantee at all.

A Culture of Complacency

It started as a little sawdust along the baseboards. No problem. A quick sweep of the broom and it was gone. A few days later, another tiny fine pile of grit. Not a problem.

And so on and so forth.

If the above sentences gave you a little jolt, I'd bet you've had a termite experience in your life. Where I live in South Florida, there are ten different kinds of termites, and the extermination companies do a booming business, as do the services that come in to repair what those tiny bugs have managed to quietly, subtly, practically invisibly tear apart.

You can have a whole termite community in your walls, a whole culture of chewing that can spit out the solidity of your home.

RUMBLE STRIPS

We mainly worry about hurricanes around here, but it's the termites that are estimated to be on track to cause 50 percent of the damage to Florida buildings by the year 2040.[8] You've got to know how to look for the signs because it's all so annoyingly subtle.

Complacency is pretty good at building its own culture, too, hiding in the walls, chewing up your resolve.

You're a leader, whether as a sole proprietor of a coaching business, an active member of your community, part of your family at home, or as a member of a multi-employee organization. Leadership leaks down to the very pores of any group. While you might not recognize shades of complacency in yourself, if you notice it in your team, if you notice it in your clients, it's there, alright. That's the dust along the baseboards.

Business economists and psychologists have put pen to paper on what complacency costs businesses each year. It's pretty startling: 60 percent of employees say they feel disengaged at work. In hard dollars, that disengagement, that lack of enthusiasm and vision and excitement, comes in at a price tag of over $7.8 trillion.[9]

That's a lot of dust, my friend.

Almost half (48 percent) of marriages that end give complacency, a lack of showing interest in each other as partners, as the reason for divorce. That makes complacency the number one reason people say their marriages fail.[10] A culture of complacency can destroy your love story.

We get complacent with our nutrition, our workouts, our friendships, our parenting. Complacency always has a cost, and far too often we seem shocked when we're handed the bill. The irony? It's not like you're just not trying.

FROM DRIFT TO DRIVE

What It Isn't

Let me share what complacency is not. It's not laziness. There are important distinctions here that I want you to consider, because often, when someone hears the word *complacency*, they equate it with not doing enough.

You won't find me telling you that you need to cram more into your days, that if you're not running at 100 miles an hour every second you're somehow doing and being less than you could. It's critical that you know that, because I would understand if you checked your schedule and duties and to-do list and calendar and walked away thinking, *Well, this calendar is the very opposite of lazy—there's no complacency to be found here!*

No, complacency doesn't mean you're not clipping through your tasks. It doesn't mean you aren't answering the emails, that you're not moving through the checklists. What it does mean is that you are simply doing these things on autopilot, no longer gauging whether all that activity and all those responsibilities and all those duties are moving you forward. You're relying on the same old methods to do the same old things, assuming you'll achieve the same old results.

Easy. Predictable. Routine.

That's not laziness. But it might be unawareness. Drowsiness at the wheel. A greater reliance on your habits than in your hallelujah.

While I understand and experience the benefits of having good habits in place, all that habit stacking might just build a wall of activity that makes it hard to see what's coming for you and blocks your view of a new possible horizon.

You're not lazy. It's just that your bar is now too low. You've worked hard to get where you are. But I want you to know this:

RUMBLE STRIPS

There are new things around the bend. New issues to address and new challenges that will require new ideas. New opportunities that can fill your heart and fuel your legacy. If you've only been about nurturing comfortable and familiar habits, when that new stuff shows up, you're going to be popping tendons faster than a backup quarterback thrown into a varsity game trying to catch up.

As American preacher and rights leader Benjamin E. Mays said, "The tragedy of life is not found in failure but complacency. Not in you doing too much, but doing too little. Not in you living above your means, but below your capacity. It's not failure but aiming too low, that is life's greatest tragedy."[11]

Hedonic...or Dynamic?

I realize that you've got a lot of voices coming at you these days, warning you about hinging all your self-worth on your accomplishments and only seeing your value through the lens of your bank statement. I know you're adding phrases and concepts to your approach to life like the *hedonic treadmill* (the phrase used to describe discontent and grasping for more stuff). There's plenty of talk today around getting away from materialism and eighteen-hour workdays and toxic work environments.

That's all great—but that's not what I'm talking about. I hope there are times when you're proud of what you've built, that you take some time to enjoy the blessings you have. I hope you are interested in being intentional about your time and your relationship to your stuff and what it all means.

When I talk about moving away from complacency, you'll

FROM DRIFT TO DRIVE

never hear me encourage you to ditch your family, ignore your marriage, compromise your physical and spiritual health, all in the name of climbing the next rung up the ladder. Not at all.

I'm challenging you to maximize who you are as a human, whatever roles you have. You've got incredible potential inside you. Moving away from complacency and toward your potential isn't about a measuring stick of going for all the toys and titles that we often allow to be the proof of our success. It's about your commitment and action toward being the best *you* you can be.

Are you willing to keep moving toward being the best leader / entrepreneur / spouse / parent / community member you have the potential to be? Or have you allowed yourself to quietly drift onto the soft shoulders of adequate, acceptable, average, and tolerable?

And how do you know if you have?

To answer that, we need to go to New Jersey.

The Garden State Parkway

Back in the 1940s, a stretch of road in Central New Jersey, Route 6 to be exact, opened with a new feature. The center line down this piece of road, dividing the lanes of traffic, looked like someone had come along with a huge bread knife and scored gashes in it, horizontal to the road's vertical direction.

Why chop up a nice smooth road with these gashes?

Because of drift.

People were drifting into oncoming traffic. Drivers were getting drowsy while on the road and losing track of where their wheels were taking them. The familiarity of the route led to the

RUMBLE STRIPS

danger of a loss of attention. The thought was that if there was something that alerted the driver to their wandering wheels, it could do a lot of good.

That little experiment in the 1940s in New Jersey led to a more concerted approach in the development of the Garden State Parkway in 1952. Rumble strips, as they became known, were a required part of that road construction. Today almost half of all rural two-lane roads and up to 90 percent of urban two-lane roads in the US have them, depending on which state you live in. It might still be that classic cuts-in-the-pavement style from the 1940s, it might be down the middle of the road or only on the shoulder, it might be the plastic or ceramic "turtle" type dots, but no doubt you've experienced rumble strips of some stripe.[12]

And they work. Rumble strips have reduced fatal rollover accidents by about 40 percent and have helped prevent drifting by 70 percent. All from a little sound or surface change along a familiar road.[13]

That's what I want to be for you in our time together, a rumble strip that wakes you up, gets you to look around, and helps you course correct.

Throughout this journey, you're going to get the tools you need to evaluate where you are. You'll work through an assessment that will uncover where you're stuck. You'll consider the symptoms of complacency, and you'll learn how to spot them in your life. You'll be equipped with a clear set of seven actionable steps to move you into realizing your greatest potential. You'll learn about different types of complacency and their causes. You'll discover how to overcome what has been holding you back.

FROM DRIFT TO DRIVE

Most importantly, you'll be reintroduced to yourself, the you who has far more to give, dream, achieve, and inspire. You'll have the tools and the plan to pull yourself back into the center lane of your purpose, your potential, and your promise to yourself to live out what's inside you.

Let's go to where we started this chapter, back to that moment in the house in the suburbs. Back to that moment with the envelope and the date set for when I had to evacuate the premises. Back to a business that failed and a market that flipped and a life turned upside down.

Like I said, on the one hand, it felt like my life was over.

But on the other, five words entered not just my head but my heart. I didn't know it at the time, but that short sentence was a battle cry against the tyranny of complacency, a mission statement that took me on a journey of personal growth, expansion of vision, and realization of potential.

I can build this again, I thought.

With those words, the smoke began to clear.

As boxing great Lennox Lewis said, "Sometimes success needs interruption to regain focus and shake off complacency."[14]

Consider this your interruption. Let's shake some things up. Because I know and, most importantly, you know, you've got more to build and more to give.

Where Complacency Hides

I was on the road with John Maxwell overseas, a speaking trip in which I was presenting to a large audience. We were in Cambodia, in a region where Khmer is the primary language. I was acclimating to the huge time change, surrounded by a language that was completely new to my ear, and quickly accommodating to some requests from the conference hosts.

As I took to the stage and began my talk, the first slide of my PowerPoint deck popped up on the huge screens. The Khmer translation for the English words on my slides was supposed to be just above my original text so the audience could understand my points in their own language. Good plan, right?

But when I glanced up at the screens as I launched into my presentation, the PowerPoint looked like someone had taken all

FROM DRIFT TO DRIVE

the elements that were supposed to be on that slide, put them in a blender on high power, dropped the blender a couple of times on the floor, and poured it all back out into PowerPoint. It was a mishmash-mess of Khmer and English and images and graphics.

Lovely.

And then the remote I was using to advance the deck as I gave my message stopped working. Just your basic professional speaker nightmare starter kit.

No problem, I assured myself. *You've presented this content plenty of times.* I made some light comedy out of the tech issues, continued my presentation, and landed the plane, so to speak. I gave myself a pat on the back as people lined up after my talk to thank me and tell me what they liked about the presentation and how great it was.

Later that evening, I went to dinner with John and a handful of colleagues.

Somewhere between our salads and our entrees, as the initial dinner chatter started to die down a bit, I pulled out a notepad and pen. "John," I began, "would you give me some feedback on my talk today?"

When I tell you he obliged me, um, yeah, he did. One observation turned to two, then turned to six. My pen flew across the page, the feedback coming fast and furious. I soon had pages of notes of John's comments. Heck, he was making it look so fun, the rest of the table started to weigh in as well. What started as a little feedback ripple became a critique tsunami.

Not exactly the "couple of pointers and let's move on to dessert" interaction I imagined.

Here's the thing: John and the dinner guests only had a couple of insights on the tech issues I'd had that day. The rest of their comments?

WHERE COMPLACENCY HIDES

They were on what I thought had gone fine, in spite of the messed-up slides and jammed clicker. That was a little tough for the old ego. None of the feedback they gave me was incorrect. And none of it was surprisingly new. What was fresh to me was the realization that some of the pointers they were giving me I had done in the past. I'd simply stopped doing some stuff that would have made the presentation better.

I hadn't stopped out of intention or an attempt to try something new. I had stopped doing those important things *simply because I had been doing them successfully for so long*. I had stopped preparing to the same level I had in the past. I was speaking from a place of the skill and development I had up to this point, but I wasn't taking as much time to prepare. It didn't show to most of the audience, but to the people who I consider some of the best of the best, well, they knew. And told me so when I asked.

I'd gone into cruise control.

If you'd asked prior to that trip if I thought I had any whiff of drift on me, I would have said categorically, absolutely, unhesitatingly, "No. Never."

And I would have believed it.

I was in my dream career, speaking and coaching for Maxwell Leadership. I was in my dream house in Florida, and Jenee and I had added three more kids to the mix, which, if you're doing the math, meant that we now had six children. I was driving my dream car, and I was living far beyond any dream I could have cooked up when I was a kid. I didn't ever want to be one to brag, but I was secretly pretty satisfied with what I'd been able to accomplish. So what if I engaged in a more plug-and-play approach these days? I'd earned it, hadn't I?

As I shared with you in the first chapter, the journey to writing

31

FROM DRIFT TO DRIVE

this book really took hold when I realized I wanted to help you, the person who finds themself drifting in the midst of accomplishment. I thought at first what I was looking at was underperformance. I had lots of different thoughts on it, ways I wanted to approach it. But during one of the brainstorming sessions, my team and I started talking about the *root cause* of underperformance.

And there it popped up again: complacency. Complacency lay at the core of so much of what we'd been talking about and exploring for the book. It was an eye-opener to me, to realize just how many places complacency touches, how it lurks at the baseboard of our plans and dreams, rotting what we thought was a solid stake in the ground.

Without even realizing I had done it, amid of getting to do so many things I had dreamed of, I'd grown complacent. Secretly satisfied with what I'd accomplished, no longer pushing and polishing to a honed point.

Once I spotted it, it lit a fire under me. It got me on a kick to search for, find, and eradicate complacency in all the areas of my life. That conversation with John and our fellow dinner partners happened during all of this. I'd been coasting, and I didn't even realize it until that very uncomfortable dinner in Cambodia. With startling clarity, I found I'd drifted from the excellence and innovation I hold in high value and exchanged it for the smug and cozy weighted blanket of "good enough."

The costs of complacency are too high for my life, and they are for yours too. Complacency will rob you of your best, it will muffle the battle cry in your heart, and it will ultimately bring atrophy to the size of your vision.

Consider this quote by Joseph C. Grew: "Moral stimulation is good but moral complacency is the most dangerous habit of mind

WHERE COMPLACENCY HIDES

we can develop, and that danger is serious and ever-present."[15]

You'd think something that dangerous and compromising to who you are would be easy to spot. But when you've had success and achievement in your life, it's not. Sure, we can pick up on one form of complacency easily enough in someone who always has an excuse, who makes big plans but doesn't see them through, who cancels meeting you at the gym, who can't show up to a meeting on time or with their presentation deck completed.

Complacency-checklist bingo right there.

No, for you and me, with the accolades and letters behind our names, complacency doesn't broadcast its presence. It's quiet. It's hidden in all the things we've done, the hard work we've completed, the projects we've seen across the finish line. David Sarnoff writes, "The great menace to the life of an industry is industrial self-complacency."[16]

We even spiritualize it sometimes, confusing complacency and contentment.

As I began to root out the complacency in my own life, I realized that I needed some tools to help me do so. Frankly, there really wasn't anything out there to aid me in determining where complacency had crept in and to what extent. I also realized I needed a tool for helping me understand the difference between complacency and contentment, and how to push out the complacency while keeping the peace of contentment.

So, over time, I developed an assessment to monitor my current levels of complacency, and it's a tool I want you to have. It's a quick way to take a reading on where you are, a series of questions to get you thinking about your life today and where you might be settling instead of excelling.

FROM DRIFT TO DRIVE

CAP: Complacency Assessment Profile

If you would like to receive a full, downloadable Complacency Assessment Profile, go to: https://drift2drivequiz.com/ or scan this QR code.

This is a tool for better understanding who you are today. This is not who you feel like you were in the early stages of your career or at the peak of your productivity and sales, so focus on who you are *right now*. Quickly move through the questions that follow and, as honestly as you can, use this scale to rate yourself:

1 – Never | 2 – Rarely | 3 – Occasionally | 4 – Always

Let's dive in:

1. Do you avoid setting new goals, either personal or professional?
2. Are you so satisfied with your current situation that you rarely look for ways to improve?
3. Do you procrastinate on tasks that could help you grow or move forward?
4. Does the thought of change feel unnecessary to you?
5. Do you often make excuses for not chasing after opportunities?
6. Are you hesitant to step outside your comfort zone?
7. Do you find yourself accepting "good enough" instead of aiming for excellence?
8. Is it hard to find the motivation to tackle new challenges?

WHERE COMPLACENCY HIDES

9. Do you feel stuck in your routine but haven't made any efforts to change it?

10. Are you quick to ignore feedback or constructive criticism?

11. Do you avoid taking risks because you're afraid of failing?

12. Has your curiosity or interest in learning new things faded?

13. Are you comfortable where you are, with no real desire to grow further?

14. Do you feel little urgency to improve your skills or knowledge?

15. Do you usually go for the easiest or least demanding tasks?

16. Do you avoid taking on new responsibilities, whether at work or in your personal life?

17. Do you feel disengaged or uninspired by what you're currently pursuing?

18. Are you leaning heavily on past achievements without striving for new ones?

19. Do you avoid thinking about areas in your life that could use improvement?

20. Is having a long-term vision or goal for your future something you tend to skip?

....

Scoring

Add up your points from your responses and see where you land:

20-30: Get Real. Come on. If no signs of complacency are showing up in your life, then why did you pick up this book? You and I both know you're feeling that something is a little off. I want to invite you to look through the assessment again and dig a little deeper (spoiler alert: almost no one gets 0–20 on this assessment. You're special… but probably not that special).

32-45: Fighting for the Wheel. Complacency is making an appearance in your life. It's time to reflect on where you can push for a bit more growth.

FROM DRIFT TO DRIVE

46–60: The Drift is Real. Complacency has you regularly hitting cruise control. It's time to revisit your goals and start taking action.

61–80: Asleep at the Wheel. Uh-oh. Complacency has fully taken the wheel and you're just along for the ride. This is your wake-up call to rediscover your passion and motivation before you end up somewhere you didn't mean to go.

How do you feel about your results? Are you surprised? A little frustrated? A little better or a little worse than you thought? Write the date next to the score explanation for your results today. This Complacency Assessment Profile is one that you can return to, even while working through this book, to continue to get a bead on how complacency is showing up for you.

Reflection Questions

Wherever you've landed on the Complacency Assessment Profile, I'd now like you to gain some further insight as to where you currently are. Take some time to reflect on the following prompts and be sure to jot down your answers. I particularly want you to pay attention to the questions that feel really hard to answer, or ones for which you don't even feel like you have an answer. Don't force yourself to answer if nothing is coming to you. Leaving something blank or struggling to pick an answer between Yes and No is an important clue into your current state. If you need to, write a question mark if you're struggling to come up with an answer.

1. When a challenge comes my way, my first thought is
   _____.

2. I've got a specific plan for personal growth that I actually stick to every week. Y or N

WHERE COMPLACENCY HIDES

3. I've found mentors or experts in key areas of my life, and I regularly connect with them for guidance. Y or N

4. In the past twelve months, I've invested in my professional growth by reading at least six books, taking classes, or listening to meaningful audio lessons or podcasts. Y or N

5. I can clearly see a road map for achieving a bigger vision for my life than what I'm currently living. Y or N

6. When obstacles arise, I don't get frustrated; instead, I see them as chances to learn and grow. Y or N

7. I make bold decisions and take personal risks that could

   _____.

8. Sometimes, I feel a vague sense of dissatisfaction but can't quite put my finger on why. Y or N

9. I'm happy with the quality of people I have in my circle. Y or N

10. I expect the people closest to me to share similar values, skills, and abilities. Y or N

11. I'm intentional about who I allow into my inner circle—both personally and professionally. Y or N

12. I meet regularly with people who challenge me to aim higher and do better. Y or N

13. I make an effort to surround myself with people who are ahead of me in life or career. Y or N

14. I welcome change and often feel restless if things stay the same for too long. Y or N

FROM DRIFT TO DRIVE

15. I'm confident in my role, even when I work with exceptionally talented people. Y or N

16. I'm willing to make personal sacrifices to_____.

17. I avoid tasks that _____.

18. I carve out time daily, monthly, and yearly to plan my schedule and prioritize what matters most. Y or N

19. I understand that trade-offs are a natural part of growth and willingly make sacrifices to become better. Y or N

20. I have a clear and strong sense of purpose that drives me to

_____.

I want to make a bold assertion here: By the end of our time together in this book, you will have a clear plan of action for being able to answer "Yes" honestly to each of the previous questions and you'll have a solid answer for each blank. Recognizing what you don't know, realizing that you're off course, is a powerful insight and an incredible opportunity for course correction.

Take a few moments to really look at those fill-in-the-blanks. What insights do you find there? I in particular find that questions 1 and 17 give me a lot of important information about my current relationship with complacency.

I'm Not Complacent, Chris. I'm Just... Content.

A friend of mine was on a road trip with some pals during college, heading to a fun weekend of events in a city a couple of hours from their college town. There was a caravan of vehicles full of fellow students driving down the highway and all was going to plan when

WHERE COMPLACENCY HIDES

one of the cars signaled that it was pulling over. A little smoke started to pool along the lip of the hood.

And then a lot of smoke.

A few of the other cars pulled over to see if they could help. Someone popped the hood, and more smoke billowed out from an engine that appeared to be glowing hot.

After some troubleshooting and the calling of a tow truck and several hours waiting and a reconfiguration of passengers, the caravan continued, minus the smoking car that rattled its way on the back of the tow truck to the nearest town and mechanic.

Days later, everyone now back on campus, a few of the friends gathered for lunch and asked the owner of the broken-down car the status of the repairs. The owner said that the mechanic reported the engine was shot and it had something to do with that genie thing.

Genie thing?

After some creative interpretation, it turned out that the owner of the car had never had the oil changed. As in, ever. And the "genie thing" was that orange-red oil can symbol that lights up on the dash when an engine is thirsty for oil (not magic).[17]

The result was that the engine burned up because it had zero oil. The car was relegated to being chopped up for parts, except for the charred engine.

So what is the "oil" when it comes to complacency? We'll get to that. Right now, I want to look at what happened to that car. There's plenty of talk these days about burnout and finding peace and being happy with what you have. I get it. After all, if you can't enjoy what

FROM DRIFT TO DRIVE

you've got, what's the point? But I've also seen contentment used as an excuse for complacence:

- **Giving the same message the same way until it becomes a reflex and not a gift.**
  But I'm "content" with the way I delivered it. It's worked fine in the past.

- **Refusing to listen to feedback or suggestions because "I've been doing this since before any of them were even out of high school!"**
  But I'm "content" with exactly how I am and how I do things, and I don't need to do anything different.

- **Stagnant production, time in the office feels boring, client interactions are adequate but not stellar.** But I'm "content" with where the business is right now.

  When you've got gifts, when you've got insight, when you've got resources, that also means you've got a responsibility to steward those things well.

  Let's run the previous statements through what a true contentment filter would look like:

- **Giving the same message the same way until it becomes a reflex and not a gift.**
  I'm content with the effort and reception this message has had in the past and I'm excited to see how I can make it a little better for the next audience.

- **Refusing to listen to feedback or suggestions because "I've been doing this since before any of them were even out of high school!"**

40

WHERE COMPLACENCY HIDES

I'm content with the accomplishments and the way I've done things up to this point and I'm open to hearing the ideas and innovations of a new generation.

- **Stagnant production, time in the office feels boring, client interactions are adequate but not stellar.**
I'm content and grateful for what I've been able to grow in business and I want to continue to offer excellence and growth in the days to come.

Different, right?

That's the next tool I want to offer you, a Contentment Versus Complacency Chart, to look at the reasons you give for places where you're not moving forward and to make sure you know the difference between contentment and complacence.

Which column of responses did you find you're using most these days? If you found yourself trending hard into the column on the far right, you may often be mixing up contentment with complacency.

In a nutshell, true contentment leads to further growth and vitality in life. Complacency makes you stagnate and prone to excuse away your lack of growth. I like the way Scott Miker explains it: "Contentment goes hand in hand with gratitude. Being appreciative of the things in your life, you see everything as a miracle. The complacent individual doesn't see anything as a miracle and takes everything for granted."[18]

I want you to have true contentment in your life, and I know that comes from living out fully all the potential you have inside you.

FROM DRIFT TO DRIVE

Contentment Versus Complacency Chart

HOW YOU VIEW:	CONTENTMENT SAYS:	COMPLACENCY SAYS:
Growth and Motivation	"I'm happy with my work/family life/relationship and I look for ways to improve and contribute."	"I've accomplished plenty, and I don't need to try harder anymore. That's someone else's problem if they don't like it."
Response to Challenges	"Sometimes the work is hard, sometimes it requires me to push myself, but I love what I do and I'm happy to be doing it."	"I'm good enough. I don't need to change anything to keep up with the times or learn any new skill. I've earned my spot and shouldn't have to do anything more."
Effort and Awareness	"While I am proud of the person I am and the things I have done, I look for further insights into what motivates me, what emotions I carry, how I respond to various situations. I'm dedicated to personal growth and insight."	"At my age, I am who I am. Take me or leave me. I'm not for everybody and I'm not going to change anything about myself. And I think a lot of that self-awareness stuff is silly anyway."
Emotional Life	"The more content I am, the more peace I have, the more I want to contribute, and the more grateful I am. Contentment is a conduit for growth."	"Sure, I'm bored. And restless sometimes. A little frustrated and irritated on the daily. But who isn't?"

WHERE COMPLACENCY HIDES

Let's go back for a moment to the car that burned out because it had no oil and the warning sign was misread. You may have been out for a proverbial Sunday drive in this season of your life, some awards and honors tucked in the back seat, humming along with a song you thought was contentment. But what if there's a quiet rumble of restlessness under the hood? What if you find that you've got a little anger or frustration that pops up on the dashboard? Or, even more significantly, what if there's some regret that's making the engine give off a little smoke?

Can we just call it what it is and what it isn't? You may have some areas of contentment in your life, and I certainly hope that you do. But there is likely some complacency hitching a ride under that contentment moniker, and the signs are there if you know how to read them.

- When was the last time you challenged yourself to do something hard?

- When was the last time you did something completely outside of your comfort zone?

- When was the last time you felt a little deliciously scared?

- When was the last time you learned something new?

- When was the last time something unexpectedly delighted you?

- When was the last time you accepted a critique meant to help you?

- When was the last time you felt fully alive and engaged and present?

- When was the last time you awakened excited and a little nervous and a lot motivated?

FROM DRIFT TO DRIVE

Over the course of the next seven chapters, you'll experience a Seven Step Framework to expose and bust through the complacency in your life. It's a road map for helping you identify what you want next and how to get there with efficiency, focus, and enjoyment. You'll learn to determine what will be most fulfilling in your next chapter and how to create a vision for that. You'll be challenged to learn in a way that allows you to onboard more information than you ever thought possible and apply that information more effectively. You'll discover how to look at your friendships and those who influence you through a new set of lenses. And you'll be equipped to take the next right steps and look at those results.

All of those things? They're oil for the engine. You're a driver. You've been to some amazing places, and you've been down some rocky roads. You're not done; you've just pulled over to a rest stop for a bit. It's not that you're unhappy, but I know you could be happier. More fulfilled. More aligned with the best of who you are. It's time to get back on the road and discover some new vistas. The next seven chapters are the hands-on, practical tools you need to get out of autopilot, take the wheel, and determine where you'll go next.

Let the drive begin.

SECTION TWO:

THE
SEVEN STEP FRAMEWORK

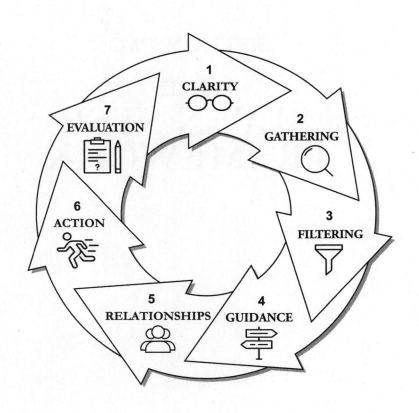

STEP 1: CLARITY
You Cannot Have What You Cannot See

There is a way for you to undo being stuck in your life, to get your tires out of the mud. Now that you have a better understanding of where things have drifted, you can begin to address the conditions that have contributed to it.

There are seven steps you can use to replace the complacency in your life with greater vitality, excitement, purpose, and meaning. I call it the Seven Step Framework. Through these steps you're going to add skills to shake out the dust and to create fresh direction. This is the framework I learned and developed through my own season of deadly drifting, the practices that helped me course correct the direction of my life. I continue to use it daily

FROM DRIFT TO DRIVE

to keep my life in the lanes that lead me to my destiny.

As you move through the upcoming chapters, it's important you keep this in mind: These steps all build on each other. You can't progress to the next one until you make the needed changes required in the step before it. It can be all too tempting to try to speed ahead, to engage in the last step or two without fully investing in the first steps. That will only lead you to shaky ground, and I want to help you build reliable highways in your life, roads that lead you to where you want to go, rather than vague side streets that wander off. So I encourage you to work through each step in sequence. That's my ask, and it's for your benefit, that you work intentionally and conscientiously through the process.

Now let's begin with the step that is often the first to go when we find ourselves marooned in the mediocre, one that can create fresh momentum.

Red and Blue Lights

Maybe you have someone in your life who, as a kid, didn't realize there were individual leaves on a tree, couldn't see the blackboard at school, had no idea that images weren't fuzzy until they got their very first pair of glasses. It's compelling to hear how someone went from a limited visual experience to a crisper, clearer world, all within the context of ground slivers of glass held in the frames of new tortoise-shell spectacles.

Me?

I've had those kinds of moments, but mine have come not while sitting in the chair at the optometrist's office but while sitting on a curb with red and blue flashing police lights pinging off my

STEP 1: CLARITY

retinas. They've come standing before a judge. They've come in the form of a question from my future wife. Those moments didn't come with a literal new pair of glasses, but they definitely put new lenses on my life, on where I was headed, on what story I would choose to live.

The way you see your life is a funny thing. In many ways, it feels like a mosaic, bits of things you've heard people say, chips of the way a teacher or friend reacted to you, fragments of beliefs and fables, all pieced and held together by a grout of guesses filling in the gaps. That potpourri of perspective combines to create your guiding principles, whether you intend for them to or not.

Growing up in Oklahoma City, and then in St. Louis, Missouri, I had lots of fragments of messages that informed my inner life. Bold as brass on the television in my childhood home were ads, PSAs declaring the lower life expectancy for Black men; that as a young Black man, I shouldn't expect to live past the age of twenty-five. What was meant to be a shocking call to action for the community simply came off as a foregone conclusion for me. That ad was my Flat Earth; my future simply slid off the edge of the calendar, nothing more to see, nothing more to explore once I hit the two-and-a-half-decade mark. That PSA was my North Star, the navigation system I took on as truth, a predominant chunk right in the center of the mosaic I called my truth.

And boy did I live it. Did I ever.

Then there were the stats thrown around about my chances of landing in jail, even if I did clear that twenty-five-year-old mortality threshold.

A lens of early death for one eye. A lens of incarceration for the

FROM DRIFT TO DRIVE

other. It meant that the line that was most clear for me to read was that I needed to get all the partying and foolishness in that I could.

That was pretty much it. After all, my expiration date was approaching.

I went to college on a baseball scholarship, but my limited field of vision kept me from performing to my potential on the diamond. The partying caught up to me quickly, as did law enforcement.

I'd been dodging speeding tickets since I first learned to drive during high school. Across the street from the mall where I held an after-school job was an attorney's office. A strip mall kind of attorney's office, no mahogany paneling, no glass and chrome conference room, just a guy I would pay to get speeding tickets taken off my record. I didn't want a bunch of consequences cluttering things up. My parents never needed to know. As far as I was concerned, no speeding tickets on my record meant they just didn't exist, that they didn't point to destructive and dangerous behavior on my part. After all, my driving record was "clean," even if it took practically all of the money I was earning at that after-school job. When the time came, I moved on to college, dragging my "clean" driving record and my bad habits with me.

Given my partying and foolishness goggles, you won't be surprised to hear that my college career was brief and bumpy. I managed to get kicked out *six* times. From the same college. If you're doing the math, that means I was somehow able to talk myself back into the same college five times. But even that admissions team had its limits.

Since a degree now seemed out of reach (another thing the stats about Black young men in America told me), I decided to

STEP 1: CLARITY

become a stockbroker. I'd heard you could make some decent money doing that, so I took the required series of tests to become licensed: the Series 7, the 63, and the 65. And sure enough, I was able to make some money as a broker, which gave me the resources for more partying and more shenanigans.

Then came the day I couldn't buy my way out of trouble anymore.

I got stopped for driving while drinking.

DUI #1.

And then came DUI #2.

While I'd somehow expensively managed to buy my way out of the first one with another strip mall lawyer, I knew the second time I was in deep. I figured it would land me in jail, just like the statistics I'd been raised on predicted. What I couldn't have predicted was Judge Daniel Pelikan.

I arrived in his courtroom ready to hear my fate. Sure enough, there wasn't a way for an attorney to get me out of a second DUI. I braced myself for what I figured would be a tirade on the judge's part about what a loser I was, what an idiot I was.

Judge Pelikan's comments started just as I expected, completely in line with those ads and those stats that framed my view. "Chris, if you keep going the way you're going, you're either going to end up dead or in jail."

Well, duh. Those were the two doors that had always been on my horizon.

"But I know you're not a dumb kid," he continued, peering at me over his readers.

Huh? What?

FROM DRIFT TO DRIVE

"It says here that you've got your broker's license. Those are hard tests to pass for anyone, and you're just a twenty-one-year-old kid. Now, you've accomplished something pretty neat here. Because you've been able to do this, I know you're not a stupid kid."

Debatable. After all, I keep getting caught drinking and driving and now I'm in a courtroom. Doesn't sound much like genius territory.

Judge Pelikan sifted through a few papers and then looked me in the eye. "So here's what I'm going to do. I'm going to do everything I possibly can to prevent you from doing this again, short of sending you to jail."

He put into motion a series of expectations and requirements to create an environment of high accountability for me. I had to blow into a tube before my vehicle would start. There were random tests I had to complete about safe driving where a device in the car would randomly beep, and I had to blow within minutes. There were courses I had to attend, including classes on the dangers of alcohol. Community service. Regular attendance at AA. He mandated the full complement.

And I did it all.

This is the part of the story where you likely expect the epic soundtrack, the soaring violins matching the revelation and light dawning in my heart. The moment the fog of uncertainty and self-sabotage lift. The kindly judge's voice becoming the angel on my shoulder, guiding and rebuilding me.

Sorry to disappoint you like a big old record scratch.

That's the thing about developing a new vision for your life. Sometimes it takes some adjustment. Sometimes it takes some getting used to. And sometimes it's a compilation of experiences, not just a singular lightning bolt.

STEP 1: CLARITY

Fast-forward a few months and I was at a Halloween party with my girlfriend, Jenee, the woman who would become my wife. We were living it up, having a time, plenty of booze to boot. When the party started winding down and it was time to leave, all those classes and requirements from Judge Pelikan *did* keep me from getting behind the wheel. Instead, it was Jenee who was driving when we got pulled over. I found myself sitting on the curb as the police officers checked our IDs and I knew, absolutely knew, that this time, I was going to jail. I'd burned through second and third and fourth chances. Even though I wasn't the person who was driving, I'd violated all kinds of aspects of my probation by my choices that night.

The red and blue lights of the police cruisers pulsed before my eyes and the vision that I'd been handed all my life, a short existence likely punctuated by periods as a prisoner, was coming true.

What does all this have to do with complacency?

Whether it's an intentional set of bad choices like in my situation or it's finding yourself stalled out in your passion and drive for life, it all comes down to this truth:

You cannot have what you cannot see.

In my case, I couldn't visualize a different future from the one the statistics had been pounding into my head since I was a kid: dead or in jail.

I'll bet there are some PSAs or billboards in your life that you've bought into, things that have come into your field of vision that are hard to see past:

- This is as high as you can go in this organization.

- If only you'd gotten that MBA.

FROM DRIFT TO DRIVE

- Women just don't get beyond this level.

- You have to choose either more success or your family; you can't have both.

- The mistakes you made years ago are going to limit your tomorrow.

- You've come to the edge of what's possible. There's no more on the other side.

- If only you'd hustled more.

- You've done plenty. Wanting more would be selfish, materialistic.

- The risks are too high to go any farther.

- You're too old for new beginnings and goals. You just need to maintain.

Any of those sound familiar? They're like the television ads that filled my field of vision as a teenager. And here's the thing: If you can't see past these things, if you can't see something fresh, you won't get there.

The Hyperopia/Myopia Paradox

In working with thousands of clients on their personal growth over the years, I've noticed blind spots that could make me something of a life optometrist. I can see signs of complacency around the edges of daily practices that are invisible to my clients. It goes like this:

Kathleen thinks she has excellent clarity on what she wants to achieve in her life. She assures me each time we meet that she is still focused on developing an e-course that is going to help lots of people and will take her consulting business where she dreams it could go.

STEP 1: CLARITY

You might take a listen to what Kathleen says and wonder, *What's the problem, Chris? Sounds like she's got plenty of clarity on what she wants to do.* Maybe. But let's look a little closer.

You see, in my sessions with Kathleen, it's always the same thing. Big dream hanging out there in the distance. Very little action in the day-to-day. Kathleen has what I call Complacency Hyperopia.

Hyperopia is a fancy optometry word that describes when someone can see things in the distance clearly but has trouble even making out the letters in the book right in front of them. That's Kathleen, alright. She can see something with more clarity off in the future, but how to get there and what she needs to do today and tomorrow and the next day are fuzzy. The common term is *farsightedness*, and she's got it bad: an overfocus on the big objective somewhere *out there* instead of a balanced focus on the important micro steps involved *today*.

Complacency Hyperopia puts you at greater risk of trying to live somewhere in the future while ignoring the importance of taking action now. That's where Kathleen's condition has landed her, in the mud of the mediocre. She misses that she's become complacent because the goal seems so big. A dream like that, with no action put to it, is simply a black hole.

If you're wondering if you might be dealing with Complacency Hyperopia, consider this: Is it easier for you to focus on a general thing you'd like to do, rather than developing the steps to get there? I find that's the case for a lot of people. They can tell me the general direction they want to go, but they really struggle with the specifics.

Some people have the opposite problem. They know what actions they want to take, but they're not really sure where they're

FROM DRIFT TO DRIVE

going. Coaching client Stephen wants to inspire people and create content. He'll spend all week researching what kind of microphone he might want to get for starting a podcast...or it could be a YouTube channel...or maybe an app with some tracks. He spends all week getting super clear on the variety of microphones out there and which ones are the most user-friendly, and which one is considered the best value, and which one is most popular with the top podcasters.

But that's about as far as Stephen ever gets. The next week he's off researching the best kind of hiking boots because maybe he should hike a mountain to inspire people and record his content from there. What kind of content? Who knows? Is there a realistic deadline for getting this content created?

Deadline? Never heard of her.

He's got Complacency Myopia, a form of nearsightedness. Where he wants to head is so vague, he simply stays back in what is easy to keep himself busy with—little details and bunny trails that have him focused more on Amazon product reviews than on actual progress.

You likely are struggling with Complacency Myopia if you find all kinds of motivation for gathering the gear, organizing your office, geeking out on the minutiae, but find yourself stalling out when it comes to being able to clearly see where all that activity is supposed to take you.

Whether you're dealing with hyperopia or myopia, my goal is to get you as close to 20/20 vision as possible, so that you can visualize with absolute clarity where you want to go and have a crisp discernment of the steps and practices that will best lead you there.

STEP 1: CLARITY

I Exam Chart

Let's use a classic eye exam tool as a way to gain clarity. You're likely familiar with what is known as the Snellen Eye Chart, an exam that starts with one large letter at the top, usually an E, and then has a series of ten more lines of letters, each line getting smaller in font size as you move toward the bottom.

I'd like for us to reimagine it as an *I* Exam Chart, where you will state what you'll do to move you toward the big idea. It's a helpful tool to take you from a general idea of what you want to do to actionable, specific goals.

Let's say you have Hyperopia Complacency, a big dream out there that you never seem able to get closer to. Maybe that dream is to one day travel internationally. That's general, the starting point—that desire to travel.

Now let's move from general to more specific. Where, specifically, would you like to go?

CHINA!

China? Great! We'll put it in a big font at the top for the big vision.

Now, let's think through specific things that will get us there. There's making sure you block the time to go. There are the finances involved—how much you can afford to spend, finding the best price for an airline ticket. You'll need to research where you're going, what you want to see, what travel arrangements you need to make. You need to be sure your passport is up to date and check with your doctor on any shots that might be required for such a trip. There's the language barrier, how you'll communicate once you're there.

These specifics start making up the rest of the I Exam Chart,

FROM DRIFT TO DRIVE

the actions that will lead you to the goal. It might look a little something like this:

Language: I will study Chinese one hour each day.

Passport: I will verify my passport status and take any necessary steps.

Travel: I will research places to visit, and book tickets and lodging.

Finances: I will save $100 every month in a travel fund for the trip.

Time: I will schedule myself as out of the office for the two weeks of the trip.

Put it all together and you've got a vision that includes both good distance and close vision:

CHINA!
Language
Passport
Travel
Finances
Time

And remember, what's near the bottom of the chart is just as important as what's at the top. These are all essential components of making your vision as crisp as possible.

STEP 1: CLARITY

Let's workshop another one, this time working it in reverse, so that if Complacency Myopia is your particular challenge when it comes to developing clarity, you can see how to find that bigger vision. Maybe you have a whole lot of small things that grab your attention, but it isn't clear how they fit together into a larger vision.

Too often we allow a lot of clutter to come into our field of vision. Imagine you visited your eye doctor and, instead of the traditional Snellen Eye Chart, she put up a chart with all kinds of big and small letters scattered all over it. And then she asked if you could see the top letter. What top letter? They're *all* up there, in all shapes and sizes. You wouldn't be able to establish a baseline and a direction. I want to encourage you to look for a singular thread to follow.

Let's explore how to do that using my coaching client Stephen as an example. All of those interests that he's chasing, they're costing him clarity. The goal with Stephen is to clear some of the letters off the chart and to get them stacked in a logical way. My recommendation to him is to pick one thing he's interested in. Let's say that of all the gear Stephen has been looking at, it's the podcast mic that gets his top vote. Great. I'd encourage him to focus on developing a podcast, picking that one medium. From there, he can begin to build a vision of what he needs to do to start a podcast. That's it. Not the YouTube channel, not yet. Not the twenty-eight-module e-course, not yet. Just the one thing. Head toward the podcast. Make that the big font at the top of the chart. Fill in the specific and important steps beneath. And get moving.

I promise you this will not limit you. In fact, it can ultimately help you move even faster.

As Drew Brees, renowned NFL quarterback writes, "When

FROM DRIFT TO DRIVE

you wake up, think about winning the day. Don't worry about a week or a month from now—just think about one day at a time."[19]

A Lens Inside a Lens

While you may find that you're specifically dealing with farsightedness or nearsightedness when it comes to what has you stuck, you might also discover that you're actually struggling with both.

I'm in a stage of life where many of my peers are starting to show up to the office in reading glasses, whereas before, they just had glasses for driving or for watching a movie on the big screen. Their close vision isn't what it used to be, and it can be tricky to accommodate for the nearsightedness they've always dealt with while also addressing this new trouble they're having with, say, being able to read messages on their phones.

Here's the good news: There's a solution called multifocal lenses, which are strategically designed for the vision correction you need wherever you are looking. They usually have a higher level of magnification near the bottom of the lens, where you likely look down when you read. Then there is a different prescription in the upper-middle portion of the same lens, calibrated to make your distance vision more crisp when you drive.

What an incredible tool for helping people with their physical vision. And what an amazing metaphor for what we need to break out of unhelpful patterns and get in the right lane.

It was a multifocal lens that helped pull me from the quicksand over twenty years ago.

There I was on the curb. Judge Pelikan had taken a chance on me, and I had blown it. An officer had Jenee a few feet away, talking

STEP 1: CLARITY

with her. The red and blue lights of the patrol cars completely filled my eyes and there was nothing more to see beyond that.

That's when I remembered a random question Jenee had asked me earlier in the evening.

"What would life be like without alcohol in it?"

I'd never considered that. Through the DUIs, I'd only been trying to figure out workarounds, ways to keep partying but to stay out of the consequences. That was what was behind my responses to Judge Pelikan's requirements, not engaging in those requirements out of improving my life, but rather staying out of his courtroom. But a life in which I didn't drink, in which I didn't even put myself in these situations?

Huh.

That was a revolutionary concept.

When I stood up from that curb, Jenee's question still rattling in my head, I'd been extended another break I can't really explain. Right before we were supposed to be loaded into a police cruiser, when the cops radioed in that they had stopped Jenee and me, one of Jenee's relatives, someone in law enforcement, heard the report. He came and picked us up, and I wasn't booked for having broken my probation.

I was given one more chance, and that night I finally had a change of view.

Clarity.

I didn't drink from that point forward. We started working on our personal growth. We started getting serious about our spiritual lives. For me, in visualizing what my life could look like without drinking, so many other things started to come into focus.

61

FROM DRIFT TO DRIVE

That's what I mean by putting on multifocal lenses. Judge Pelikan gave me a picture of what was going to happen if I didn't pull myself together. And he also helped me see that I wasn't a dumb kid, that I did have something to offer, that I did have a different future available rather than the one I was living. While that vision wasn't quite enough to pull me out of my current patterns, it did begin to shine a little light out ahead. And when Jenee asked me, "What would life be like without alcohol in it?" a whole new panorama opened up.

Think about creating greater clarity in your life, making you more adept at spotting complacency and stamping it out, whether it's out in the distance or up close.

The Everest Problem

Okay, Chris, all well and good. But I was able to attain my goals. I've got a consistent track record. I was pretty good at holding the general direction and the specific steps in focus at the same time. I aced the I Exam Chart back in the day. My issue now? I just don't know how to create a new vision. I don't have a passion project, a line pulling me toward something. Is that still complacency? And how do I fix that?

Great questions. Truly. I do encounter people who haven't had trouble in the past with Complacency Hyperopia or Complacency Myopia. They've simply arrived at a stage in their lives where they've accomplished what they set out to do and they feel like there's nothing of interest left to conquer.

What do I tell them?

Get into a new environment.

It's one of the most powerful things you can do, to expand your vision of what's possible.

STEP I: CLARITY

Let me give you a real-time example.

I'm a guy who likes cars. That is, I can appreciate a really nice car. I can't tell you what makes an engine special or anything like that, but I do enjoy a quality leather seat and a great sound system. That kind of guy. You likely have been picking up on that, given my frequent references to driving and many of the metaphors throughout this book. I feel like most everyone has their thing, whether that's a certain kind of handbag they value, or a travel experience, or being able to have a series of apartments in the cities where their grown kids are living.

Remember how I've talked about the limited vision I was offered about what my life as a young Black man in this country would entail? It wasn't just the television commercials and dismal statistics. It was also the messaging I received from really well-intentioned people.

When I was about twelve years old, one of my best buddies came from a family who were a few clicks up the economic ladder from mine. He had a bedroom to himself, a real bedroom. He'd been to my house before and when I took him to my bedroom, he asked why my bedroom door had two doors that folded back on themselves. I thought it was such a weird question. "Those are just the doors that came with my bedroom," I told him. He didn't say anything more about it.

It wasn't until I went to his family's home and saw his bedroom that I realized something: My bedroom was a closet. Those doors to my bedroom were bifold closet doors. His bedroom was roomy and had one door, a solid door, that closed it off from the hallway. His family had some appliances I'd never encountered. They had snacks,

FROM DRIFT TO DRIVE

snacks that were brand names, and they had a lot of them. His dad came home from work in a suit and tie, still smelling of aftershave, no oil or grime beneath his nails like my dad had when he came home from a shift at the General Motors plant.

My friend's lifestyle seemed magical to me, even though now I realize it was a pretty average middle-income household.

One day, his mom was driving my friend and me somewhere near the Crossroads Mall in Oklahoma City, on I-35. I heard a low growl coming up from behind us, and suddenly, powering past us in the other lane, a gleaming white Camaro came rumbling up on the driver's side, swinging past in a blur of horsepower and cool vibes.

"Wow," I breathed. "Man, I want one of those." My heart beat a little faster as the Camaro pulled far ahead, its shining bumper winking at us in the sunlight.

My friend's mom sighed. "Oh, Chris, honey," she explained, "you and your family won't ever be able to afford one of those cars."

Now, I want to be clear, this was someone who cared about me. I think she was trying to do what she thought was most compassionate, to mitigate potential disappointment in my life. She likely was speaking out of a motive of wanting me to be "realistic," to understand the realities of economics and scarce opportunities and how the level required to get a car like that was going to be far beyond my reach.

Like I've told you, I believed the television ads about my life expectancy, and I believed the stats that said I'd likely end up in jail. But for some reason, the idea of owning that Camaro, the vision that I could figure out a way to have a car like that, it simply wouldn't bend to the limited roofline my friend's mom presented to me.

64

STEP 1: CLARITY

The first car I bought when I got my first sales job?

You guessed it.

A Camaro.

My vision was expanded that day on I-35 near the mall. If I want to get really poetic, since it was near the Crossroads Mall, I'd say that was a significant crossroads for me that day. Ready for a little more poetry? Like I mentioned, my dad worked at a GM plant. And guess what? GM produced the Camaro.[20] But the jump between being part of a manufacturer that built those cars and owning one wasn't a horizon line I ever heard talked about in my house. It was a leap I had to make through a new clarity of what was possible.

Over the years, cars have been a visible measure of where I'm at in my career, where I'm achieving certain goals, where challenges have to be overcome. As you know from an earlier chapter, I had a time where I had to turn my cars back over, when our house was foreclosed on, and I had to start over. I've had not just one, not just two, but several of my dream cars tucked in the garage at night.

For me, they're always a symbol of moving past the limited field of vision I was presented with as a twelve-year-old.

And I would have told you, based on the cars I'm currently driving and enjoying, that I fulfilled the vision. Dusted and done.

Until...

I recently met a new friend. As he and I chatted, and he realized how much I love fancy cars, he whipped out his phone to show me something.

It was a garage, newly constructed at his home. And in that sparkling, customized garage were *fourteen* supercars, all parked in an absolute dream space for any of us who bear such automotive love.

FROM DRIFT TO DRIVE

I've got to tell you: I was rocked in the best way. It was a white-Camaro-on-the-interstate moment, a vision for what's possible. Here was someone gifting me with a bigger vision than I'd previously had. In one snapshot, he put me into a different environment, and it yanked my wheel back into a lane of growth.

I don't tell you all this to get you to focus on something material or to put you in a headspace to try to keep up with the Joneses. Not at all. What I'm talking about is something far more important. It's about exposing your mind to bigger and bigger vistas of *what's possible*.

As a whole when it comes to physical eyesight, our society is becoming more and more nearsighted. The current estimates are that about 30 percent of the world's population is nearsighted and that the percentage will jump to 50 percent by 2050.[21] The rates are statistically growing very quickly here in the US, and it's far worse in China. I recently learned through a podcast that this is because we're spending more and more time focused on screens. We're spending more and more time indoors, where our eyesight is limited to the four walls that surround us. And even if we do go outdoors, if we're living in high-rise cityscapes, it means that we're still not using our vision to look at things that are distant, far from where we currently stand.

The podcast guest, Dr. Joseph Allen, who is an optometrist, explained that it's thought that nearsightedness is growing worse here in the States because we're letting our kids get on screens at earlier and earlier ages, and therefore they aren't using their vision to spot things on the horizon. In China, because so many people live in urban settings in which they can only look out at the next high rise and the next, their vision acuity continues to drop.[22]

STEP I: CLARITY

It got me thinking about you, about me, about how we lose our figurative sight once we've accomplished some things about what could be next. When you've achieved success in your life, when you've gotten to your destination, it can be all too easy to decide that there's nowhere else to go.

Sir Edmund Hillary was a guy who knew something about getting to the top. He and mountaineer Sherpa Tenzing Norgay scaled Mount Everest in 1953, the first confirmed climbers to summit.[23] Could there be a bigger goal than Everest? Um, no. After all, Everest is the highest point on Earth.

But Hillary had a bigger vision than just that peak. As part of his time traveling to Tibet, preparing for his climb, interacting with other climbers and local people, he developed a new vision for what was possible. For his next mission, he established the Himalayan Trust. This organization helped develop schools and hospitals in Nepal. It brought fresh water to communities. It established vaccine programs. The Trust built an airstrip for bringing in needed construction supplies. Every goal that Hillary set for the area would reveal new challenges, which would create an ever-expanding vision.

Today, the Himalayan Trust continues to grow and operate in the area, including providing relief efforts in the devastating earthquake that hit the region in 2015.[24] It's a humanitarian peak of compassion beyond the peak Hillary originally climbed. All because one guy who scaled the world's tallest mountain decided to not let that be the ceiling of his vision. He refused to let complacency of his accolades restrict his sight.

You can stay nearsighted on Everest.

FROM DRIFT TO DRIVE

Or you can develop 20/20 vision for your next chapter, a chapter built of your expertise, your experience, your knowledge, your heart.

Get yourself into some new environments. Ask for a coffee with a person who has gone a little farther, who has pushed a little higher. Go to the conference with the people who have achieved more than you thought possible. Sign up for the marathon, the climb, the event that makes you push yourself and stand shoulder to shoulder with others who can see a little farther and a lot more clearly than you.

Complacency resides in a silent confusion about what to do next. Clarity weeds complacency out of the path. Ask yourself the hard questions, elevate your eyes, and focus on a new horizon. It's there, alright, ready for you to discover.

STEP 2: GATHERING
Learn a Little,
Do a Little

Imagine that you are craving something sweet. Something that has a crumbly texture to it. Something that also has a layer of icing that has a bit of a crunch. You know the texture and the flavor of what you're wanting.

So you head to the kitchen. And you stand there at the kitchen island, waiting for it to appear. After all, you've got clarity on the key components of what you want to experience. You're ready for it to show up.

You stand there. And you stand there. And you stand there.

Or let's say that after you visualize the flavor and texture of this dish you're wanting, you head to the kitchen and start pulling every

FROM DRIFT TO DRIVE

ingredient you can think of out of the cabinets. Every seasoning. Every bag of flour. Every bottle of oil and vinegar. Every cut of meat in the freezer and every block of cheese and every egg. You throw all of that on the island, get you a big mixing bowl, and randomly stir all this stuff together.

I hate to disappoint you, but at the end of either scenario, you're not going to get what you hope for. There is likely a recipe, a shopping list, and a process to follow for whatever outcome you want to achieve. But if you don't gather the information and necessary ingredients (and *only* the necessary ingredients), you'll find yourself standing at either an empty kitchen island or one that looks like a culinary explosion.

While getting clarity on what you want to achieve next is such an incredibly important first step, it can also be a step where we can, once again, fall victim to complacency and get stuck. We either don't start moving in the direction of our vision, or we start to willy-nilly throw anything and everything at it. That's why moving out of complacency isn't a one-step process; it's a seven-step process, and each step is critical to moving you high above the valley of complacency.

This next step reveals both your next move forward and where you may have gotten stuck in the past.

Gathering.

Gathering is intentionally pulling together resources, input, training, experiences, and ideas to guide you in your lane. This is where you begin compiling books, audiobooks, lectures, videos, and conversations to help supply you with what you need to journey toward your goal. Gathering helps keep the flame burning with your

STEP 2: GATHERING

passion. It sets the stage for determining your next steps. Think of this as a research phase, when you're discovering wisdom and insights for where you're headed next.

You have to know more before you grow more.

I get so excited about Gathering because I know that information invites growth. When I embraced gathering, it changed the direction of my life and career. Gathering expands your world, what you notice, what you observe. You can make more confident decisions when you've gathered great information. You'll have a deeper understanding of your world, of what makes you tick, of what helps others. Over time, what you gather becomes part of you, becomes part of the wisdom and experience you have to offer. Gathering is a superpower!

Remember where we ended the last chapter, high up on Everest, peering with Sir Edmund Hillary at what the next peak and the next peak could be? Exciting stuff, right? But here's the part in our journey where I have to warn you about the potential dangers that come when you head out into a new adventure, into a new vision.

When I talk about this step of Gathering, I always say that it's the most dangerous transition point between all the steps. I find that people usually fall into one of two categories: They consider themselves action people and want to skip information gathering altogether, or they are perpetual information gatherers who never want to stop hunting. People can either get overwhelmed here or trapped. That's because there's a metaphorical monster that roams the halls.

FROM DRIFT TO DRIVE

The Complacency Hydra

The Greeks had a mythological monster that appeared in some of their stories, a beast called the Hydra. It had one body and lots of heads. Some writers said it had six heads, some said nine, others fifty. In a lot of the ancient tales in which the Hydra appears, the hero of the story is on a mission to vanquish the monster, but each time the hero cuts off one of the heads, another one appears. It takes some special techniques and strategies (and a magic sword or two) to finally defeat the Hydra.[25]

Complacency in the Gathering step is a lot like the Hydra. You see, about the time you think you've defeated it, you learn that you've simply conquered one face of it and that there is still some battle to go.

I tell you this not to frustrate you but to equip you. I promise you, I'm someone who doesn't spend much time thinking through bad news or worst-case scenarios or negativity. Do I know those things exist? Sure. But I'm far more interested in solutions and growth and progress than sitting around pondering what could go wrong or could be hard.

So when I tell you that you'll likely find some challenges with gathering because complacency is something of a Hydra, I do so to equip you well, to bring your blade to each stop on our journey together. The steps of overcoming drift that we're working through are absolutely a road map for guiding you away from complacency and into growth. And these steps are also the places where people run off into the ditch. Hence this warning sign: Monsters Ahead.

Let's take on the four most common faces of the Complacency Hydra.

STEP 2: GATHERING

Face #1: DIYing to the Death

Jenee and I were getting ready for our move to Florida after I had happily accepted the position of Executive Vice President of The Maxwell Leadership Entrepreneurial Solutions Group. In the process of selling our home in St. Louis, we wanted to make sure the house was in tip-top shape for the next family. We had some small nail holes in the walls from pictures and artwork we had hung around the house. My buddy Matt, who is a professional residential and commercial painter, came by the house one day, patched up some nail holes and touched up one room for us, showing me how he did things. By the time he wrapped up and left that day, that room looked good as new.

I should have hired him to take care of the rest of the house. But that DIY spirit showed up. *Didn't look that hard*, I thought. *I can brush over some nail holes.* I would be DIY King by sundown.

We had only enough leftover paint in the garage to touch up the one room that Matt took care of, so I made my way to the paint store and got some more of what looked like the same color. I got back to the house and raced around each room with my magic paint brush, eliminating any evidence of patched nail holes. When I tell you that when I finished I had a sense of significant DIY pride, I mean it.

Which was all well and good. Until the paint actually dried.

Well, that doesn't look right…

Everywhere that I had touched it up, you could tell. The wall texture looked different. The paint color looked slightly off. And why were all those places I touched up…dull?

It was Matt who came back to the house to save the day. As

FROM DRIFT TO DRIVE

it turned out, in all of my enthusiasm to tackle this project myself, I'd missed some important information. First of all, when those nail holes were filled, the putty needed to dry and then needed to be lightly sanded. I missed that point.

Then I learned that paint comes in all kinds of finishes. And what brand you choose matters. Who knew? Not me. And I'd managed to pick up a paint that was a primer, not a finishing paint. I'd also only put one coat on, when at least two were needed. I'm sure there was also something in there about techniques and feathering the finish and all sorts of other details. Matt got my mess cleaned up and I learned an important lesson about gathering that day.

There are all kinds of people who have spent all kinds of time developing the expertise you need to get back on track toward your vision. And when they're really good at what they do, it can look effortless. Easy. That was my mistake with my friend Matt. He made it all seem so simple that I missed the nuance.

When it comes to Gathering, I want to challenge you to ditch any kind of a spirit of pride that makes you think you know better than someone who has gone before you. Keep your confidence; I feel certain you can do what you put your mind to. But the right posture is to know that you don't know everything and that the information and resources and insights from others who have gone before you are mission critical.

Face #2: So Special

*Okay, Chris, I hear you. But what I want to do is so unique, so revolutionary, so **special**, that no one has gone where I'm going.*

This is the next face of the Complacency Hydra, the one where

STEP 2: GATHERING

you think what you're envisioning is different enough that you need to create completely new procedures and approaches to make it happen.

My wife and I have a newly discovered love for hiking. I booked us a trip to the mountains, up in the Rockies of Colorado, and the hiking was incredible! We talked; we climbed in the quiet; we saw incredible views of the mountain peaks and dramatic landscapes. After that, my radar was switched on for all things hiking and mountains and Colorado, and I ran across an interesting article. Two of the airports considered the most dangerous in the world are in Colorado.[26] This is not because they have dismal safety statistics; not at all. As a matter of fact, it's considered something of a badge of honor, a mark of a superior pilot, to land planes in Aspen and in Telluride, both in the Centennial State. What makes those two airports the most challenging is the fact that they are both high up in the mountains, where weather and winds can be unpredictable. The airport at Telluride is the highest in the United States. And both airports have short runways, surrounded by the craggy peaks of the mountains, making the level of challenge all the greater.

Now, imagine the pilot decided that, because these locations are so different from most other airports, he's going to fly in for the first time without consulting any of the accrued aviation knowledge. What would we think of this pilot if he said, "This flight is so special, this destination is so specific, I don't need to consult pesky things like weather radars and physics. I'm going to create a completely revolutionary approach"?

You wouldn't find me in that plane, even with the promise of great hiking on the other side of that flight. A great pilot needs,

FROM DRIFT TO DRIVE

yes, a clear vision of where he's headed. And he may indeed develop safer and better techniques for landing at challenging airfields. But he's also a great pilot because he understands there is wisdom that is applicable to his destination.

The author Samuel Clemens (who we know as Mark Twain) was asked by Congress to give his thoughts about extending copyrights for authors. As he was traveling by train to testify before Congress on the issue, he and his traveling companions were talking about originality. Clemens summed up his thoughts by saying, "There is no such thing as a new idea. It is impossible. We simply take a lot of old ideas and put them into a sort of mental kaleidoscope. We give them a turn and they make new and curious combinations. We keep on turning and making new combinations indefinitely; but they are the same old pieces of colored glass that have been in use through all the ages."[27]

While I don't doubt that you've got an original way of communicating and problem-solving and helping people, a way that is part of the vision you have, it doesn't mean that you can't draw important, applicable strategies and tools from others' experiences. What it does mean is that I want you to focus on gathering information toward accomplishing your vision from a place of understanding the value of what you're offering, rather than overemphasizing its "new" or "revolutionary" nature.

In an *Inc. Magazine* article by Stephen Shapiro, I found this amazing quote from Mark Bowden, the founder of Truthplane.[28] He says, "I suspect part of the problem is in the word 'original' being thought to mean new, rather than to mean 'now seen from over the horizon.' We don't look over the curvature of the earth to notice the

STEP 2: GATHERING

new day was already there. We are quite obsessed with the value of 'newness.'"[29]

Someone has likely developed a speaking career around a topic you are passionate about. Someone has likely built a successful coaching business similar to what you envision. Someone has probably started a brick-and-mortar organization like the one you have a vision for. This is not a signal to stop. You will bring something original and new to the table because your experiences and personality and drive are not going to be the same as someone else's. However, this also means that you have things you can learn from others, no matter how much of a fresh perspective you carry in your vision.

How does someone who has tackled a similar problem to the one you want to solve work? What are the tools they've used? How do they organize their time, their workspace?

Don't be fooled by the face of the Complacency Hydra that tries to convince you that there's no information out there that will be helpful in your quest because your idea is too original or special. There's always something to learn.

Face #3: More, More, More

Remember Stephen from the previous chapter, the guy with Complacency Myopia who kept chasing the next shiny object? His form of gathering was trailing after whatever caught his attention in his immediate line of sight. But that kind of gathering had little focus on where he wanted to go and what he wanted to accomplish, with clarity, out in the future.

Stephen would also likely be a prime victim for this next face of the Complacency Hydra, the head I think of as More, More, More.

FROM DRIFT TO DRIVE

This head of the Hydra tries to convince you that you can't move forward if you don't have *all* the information, if you haven't researched *all* the things. It's the polar opposite of Faces #1 and #2 and yet the net result is pretty much the same: You stay stuck. It tries to convince you, even after you've chosen a lane, that you can't move forward until you know every single detail. But if you allow gathering to turn into an all-consuming information hunt, an end in itself, that's all you will have accomplished. I call this Gathering Overdrive, and now more than ever before, with the world's knowledge at your fingertips on your phone, if you think you have to exhaust every avenue of available information, that's all you'll ever be doing.

While you won't find it among his writings, Will Rogers, the legendary actor, humorist, and social commentator, is often credited as saying, "Even if you're on the right track, you'll get run over if you just sit there."

If there is one place in this book that I'd want you to highlight, it's this next line.

Are you ready?

Here it is:

Learn a little, do a little.

You're going to see this maxim of "learn a little, do a little" show up time and again throughout this book. It's been one of the most important directives in my own career building and complacency busting.

That's a powerful practice in the art of Gathering. We're going to gather a little. And then, we're going to learn a little. And then try it. And then gather a little more and learn a little more. And then try that. We'll be engaging the next step as part of this practice, where

STEP 2: GATHERING

you'll learn solid methods for learning and for application. You don't have to have everything you'll ever need toward your pursuit all gathered at one time. It's a process, gathering some information, then processing it for use. It's the way you once and for all lop the #3 Face of More, More, More off the Complacency Hydra.

Why is it so powerful? Because it maximizes the step of gathering with action. In upcoming steps, you'll learn more about how to effectively do this, but for now, I want you to commit this line to memory, because it deeply informs the *why* of gathering:

Learn a little, do a little.

The reason I see people get stuck fighting the Complacency Hydra head of More, More, More is because I think we want to be seen as "the expert," even when we're getting started on a new venture. As my work colleague and friend Lorna likes to say, you learn by doing. You aren't going to be the expert starting out on this new vision, and that can be particularly tough when you've been seen as an expert in previous endeavors.

I have a friend who has been in the process of getting twins through the driver's education process and getting their licenses. (I'm taking notes since we're starting the driving thing with our triplets. Three kids all learning to drive at the same time. Say a prayer for us.) My friend shared with me that, even though one of the twins has now had her license for a few months, she'll often put her "Please Be Patient. Student Driver" magnet on the car when she's driving to a new area of town or into a tricky parking situation. My friend told me how inspiring they find this to be. "I don't think I would have done that as a teenager," my friend confessed. "I wanted everybody to see me as older than I was, that I was an expert driver and on and on. But I love that she's like, no, I'm still figuring this out."

That's the mentality I want you to take as you work through the gathering process. You'll add a little information a little at a time, with a little more experience. Put a bright yellow magnet up in the corner of your mind to be patient with yourself, that you're a student in this. Gather a little and learn.

Face #4: Again?

For the most part, when you think about the step of Gathering, I do want you to think about gathering information and resources associated with your vision. But there is something you need to gather that's a little more subtle, while just as important.

It won't surprise me at all if, after you've worked through the first step of Clarity, and as you're working through the step of Gathering, conquering the faces of the Complacency Hydra in your path, that there's one more face you will likely struggle with. This is particularly true if you've accomplished many of your previous goals, if you've achieved a certain status.

I have found that very successful people have a particularly tough choice to make when it comes to overcoming complacency. The restart is hard because you've got to make a choice to pay the price again. You've got to make a choice to change priorities again. You've reached a place of comfort, and you've got to decide if you're willing to change your habits, your environment, and your priorities.

The Complacency Hydra will come at you saying, "Again? Are you really willing to start over again, now that things are easier? Are you really willing to do what it takes?"

STEP 2: GATHERING

Which is why I want to encourage you to *gather your resolve.* Your reason why. Your passion. It's all too easy to get fired up and excited in the Clarity phase. But when you start to gather what you need, the reality starts to set in. So, in addition to the wisdom and resources you're gathering, gather your strength. Decide, really decide, that you'll move through all seven steps, not just these first couple. And I have to tell you, particularly when you've built other businesses and achieved other goals, this might not be the last time in this journey the "Again?" face of the Complacency Hydra will taunt you. When challenges come (and they will), when you're tired, when you want to cut corners, you may find yourself thinking, *Should I really be trying this again?* Each time it shows its face, be ready with the passion you have to take this new peak. Gather that resolve and keep it close, every step of the way. Resolve is the blade that cuts through all doubt.

Putting It All Together

You've got your mindset ready. You know there's always something to learn. You understand that while your vision is unique, there is wisdom to glean. You know that you don't have to have all the information in this first round of Gathering, and you've got your resolve ready to go. Excellent.

At this Gathering stage, there's something I've intentionally omitted, and I wonder if you've noticed. With Gathering, note that I haven't told you to *start* reading or listening or processing just yet. Sometimes when I find someone who is stuck in the Gathering stage, it's because they've gathered one book and they're reading it all the way through before they gather another book. That's our next step.

FROM DRIFT TO DRIVE

I have specific tools to guide you in moving through all of the information you've gathered. Trust me, that time will come. But at the Gathering stage, you're doing precisely only that: collecting resources that you think might inform where you want to head.

Let's put it in big letters:

THIS IS GATHERING. Not reading, listening, processing, not yet.

You're curating a collection of things that you have reason to believe will give you direction and ideas for your steps forward. The goal is not that you will only have things in your basket that are 100 percent applicable. The goal is to gather what seems like it has potential to be of value to that goal you've developed clarity for.

How do you go about gathering these things? I like to think of it by the acronym BVACC, which stands for Books, Videos, Audio, Coaching, and Courses. Here are some ideas on how to start:

- Find someone who is accomplishing (or has accomplished) something similar to what you want to accomplish, and ask them what they're reading and listening to.

- Create playlists of podcasts in your area of interest. You can also include podcasts about building good habits, overcoming procrastination, marketing insights, and more.

- Gather books that are topical to your vision.

- Search online booksellers for resources that match keywords to your objective.

- Pull articles, videos, and lectures that are suggested in the "You Might Also Enjoy…" features of online resources.

STEP 2: GATHERING

- Look for classroom, online, and video-based courses and seminars associated with your area of focus.

- Overall, only look for things that tie directly to what you are trying to achieve.

I want to push you to gather ten resources before we move on to the next step. Why ten? Here's the answer, along with some other things to look for in the resources you seek out.

Enough: If you tend to fight the More, More, More face of the Complacency Hydra, ten will give you a helpful stopping place. Ten resources are plenty of content to move on to the next step without being overwhelming.

Avoid the One and Done: If you invest in one book or one course and stop there, you may become convinced that it's the only way. You become overly reliant on one source and don't take advantage of the incredible bounty of wisdom available from other places.

Simple: Don't skip something because you think it sounds too simple. This is a mistake I often see people make, that if a resource isn't pages and pages long, or if the podcast is only ten minutes, they'll skip past it, thinking it won't be meaty enough. One of the most important life-changing resources I've ever encountered, one that deeply impacted how I learn, was a seven-minute-long video on YouTube (I'll share about it in the next chapter). Short and simple content can hold absolute treasure.

83

FROM DRIFT TO DRIVE

Specific: Gathering is powerful and it's *specific*. It's not about bundling up everything that looks interesting. It's about finding things that might be in the lane that you've envisioned for yourself. If you find you are collecting things that run the gamut, you likely don't have the level of clarity that you need for this step. Go back to the previous chapter and run the play again. Choose one thing. Gather for one thing. Leave all the other shiny objects for another day.

Mindset: Gathering requires consistency, open-mindedness, and curiosity. Some people are natural gatherers; they've always got their radar on for things that speak to their passions. Other people spend fifteen minutes on a random Monday looking up a couple of books and then move on to other things. A few months later, they find themselves no closer to their goal, and they haven't added anything to their storehouse of knowledge. It's important to frame gathering as a specific commitment on your calendar. Block out time that you will commit to seeking resources. Gathering is not an aside; it's deeply intentional.

When we move on to the next step, and you dig more deeply into what you've gathered, you're going to find some things that are absolute bullseyes. You're also going to find some things that are misses. That's okay. There's something to be learned from those as well.

One of my favorite teachers, Jesus, told a parable about a man who had planted a field of wheat. During the night, some enemies of this man came to his field and threw in seeds for weeds. When the crop started to grow, the man's workers realized there were weeds among the wheat. They asked the man if they should start pulling

STEP 2: GATHERING

out the weeds, but he told them to wait, that they might accidentally pull out the good wheat. When it came time to harvest the wheat, that's when they could separate the weeds from the wheat.

That's where we're headed next, a step to help you learn, process, remember, and keep what adds up to the harvest you want to see. Right now, focus on keeping your curiosity high and your resolve firm. Learning a little, doing a little, you're building a recipe for success.

STEP 3: FILTERING
How to Find the Gold

....

I can tell you the math equation that separated me from the success I wanted to experience.

55 inches > 800 square feet

Um, Chris? I think you might have that backward, buddy.

Technically, sure. But when it comes to getting to where you want to go, shaking the dust of complacency out of your life, that's a math equation you want to remember.

After I'd gotten kicked out of college for the last time (the *sixth*, remember?), I figured I needed a job. And when the following opportunity popped up, I jumped on it:

Are you interested in a fun atmosphere that doesn't have the same

FROM DRIFT TO DRIVE

work environment every single day?

Yes.

Do you like to travel?

Yes.

Are you young and ambitious?

Yes and yes!

What an opportunity! And if you thought to yourself, *Wow! That job description sounds like selling perfume and cologne out on the street every day*, then you would be correct. That's what I did: perfume and cologne sales out in the wild, a different block of the city with each sunrise. While I didn't find the perfume industry to be my calling, the experience I picked up in that role created an important shift in my world. It was like a magic pill.

What would you say if I told you this magic pill would cut your risk of developing dementia by 250 percent,[30] would add at least two years to your lifespan,[31] would reduce your stress levels by 68 percent,[32] and would increase your income,[33] and that I had the data to back up all these claims?

You'd say, "Give me that pill!" Right?

But every day, I encounter people who say they won't take the "medication," that they don't have time for it or they're not interested or they find it boring.

The magic pill?

Reading.

It was a pill I myself had avoided.

In that short-lived job of selling perfume and cologne, every day that I came to work to pick up my wares, the team leader would read a chapter from Napoleon Hill's classic *Think and Grow Rich*

STEP 3: FILTERING

before we headed out to sell. For me, it was the first time I'd ever worked through a book start to finish.

And, yes, I had already graduated from high school, and yes, I'd already put in some time at college. Up to this point, I hated reading, didn't see the point of it, and had relied on my athleticism to carry me through my academic career. But now, I started to experience the value of reading. I realized that the ideas in that book were making their way into my mind. And my mind was making use of those ideas in ways I'd never thought of before.

While I moved on from in-the-street perfume sales pretty quickly, the practice of reading and the content of *Think and Grow Rich* impacted me deeply. I picked up other sales jobs along the way, everything from furniture and futons to stocks, bonds, insurance, and mutual funds; you name it, I sold it. Ultimately, it led me to working at a call center offering extended warranties to customers, where my previous sales experience equipped me for hitting some epic sales numbers.

I was twenty-one years old, making over $100,000 a year. Living the dream.

But there were other people up the ladder from me, and I started thinking about what it would be like to have one of their jobs, to teach other people to make the kind of sales I was making. I didn't really have a phrase to describe what I wanted to do, to better myself to take on higher roles in the company, but I knew I wanted to learn more. It was my first intentional jump into what I would later understand to be personal growth, and that jump landed me in a church basement, watching John Maxwell leadership training videos every Tuesday evening.

FROM DRIFT TO DRIVE

Now I was hungry to learn more.

In 2004, several years after the perfume job, I attended a conference at which Dr. Dennis Kimbro was the keynote speaker. Dr. Kimbro had been contracted to rewrite Napoleon Hill's *Think and Grow Rich* work from an African American perspective. As part of that project, he interviewed numerous African American millionaires, and at the conference, he shared what he'd learned.

Many things he said in his message have stuck with me through the years, but one point really hit home.

"I had the opportunity to interview all these millionaires," Dr. Kimbro shared. "And when I went to the houses of these millionaires, I began to recognize something. The larger the house, the fewer the number of TVs and the smaller the TVs."

Wait. What?

He continued, "And then I went into lower-income houses. What I discovered is that when I went into smaller houses, I found larger televisions. The larger the house, the smaller the square inches of TV. The smaller the house, the larger the square inches of TV."

At that moment I came to an emotional traffic jam. I call it my TV Turnaround. In that moment I knew that I had a problem. I was living in an 800-square-foot apartment with a 55-inch TV, and not a book to be found. I had unintentionally embraced the math of small living and small thinking, while those who had achieved what I dreamed of played by a different equation.

That was the math: making 55 inches of television greater than 800 square feet of living space. My ratios were all off. My focus on entertainment and wasting my time was greater than my desire to grow. If I continued with that math, the walls of my limited

90

STEP 3: FILTERING

understanding were going to close me off from my potential. It was all right there in the math of my priorities.

I knew something needed to change. I knew that I needed to do something different.

And that's when my passion for reading fully ignited.

The Book Haters Club

You've collected the ten resources described in the second step, Gathering. And now you've arrived here with a pile of things to work through.

Books. Articles. Transcripts.

It's one thing to gather resources, like you did with the previous chapter.

And it's another thing to start reading.

When I speak on the importance of reading, I often begin by asking people their top reasons for not reading. You'd be amazed at how many people have all kinds of reasons for why they don't pick up a book as part of their plan for moving toward their goals:

I don't like reading.

I'm a slow reader.

I'm too busy to read.

Reading is boring.

Not to brag, but I've already been the president of all of those book-hater clubs. As I've told you, I hated reading in school. I was a very slow reader and was consistently frustrated at how long it would take me to read something I was forced to read. Then, as I was starting my career and as Jenee and I started our family, I thought I was far too busy to take time to read. I also served as the president

FROM DRIFT TO DRIVE

of the Reading Is Boring Club, not stopping to consider that the boredom might have more to do with *what* I was trying to read than the practice of reading itself.

Look, I've got to think you're something of a reader since you've picked up this book. You've made it to this chapter, so you must find value in the content. And I get that perhaps this book is the exception for you, that you don't consider yourself much of a reader. However you find yourself here, as a book lover or as someone who is struggling, this step is a critical one. Whether you already appreciate the value of books or it's new to you, I'm going to equip you with tools to be able to read more, to gain more value from what you read, and to retain the important guidance, ideas, inspiration, and strategies from what you've gathered.

We're all consuming content somewhere. We're scrolling the web, getting lost in our favorite social media apps, and hitting all those streaming platforms available to us 24/7. The average American today spends thirty-three hours a week watching television.[34] Thirty-three. Hours. That's practically another full-time job! I want to really push you at this point to consider the content you are consuming. Are you taking in things each week that will move you closer and closer to the vision you have for yourself? Or are you spending a chunk of time watching fictitious people in fictitious places doing fictitious things? Listen, I love some couch-rotting time on occasion, bingeing a television series. But a steady diet of the stuff isn't going to equip you or take you where you want to go.

If you think you don't like reading, let's try again with the information you're going to gain from this chapter. If you think you're a slow reader, I have some great help on the way for you. If you think

STEP 3: FILTERING

you're too busy to read, no, you're not. I'm going to share how to exponentially move through the content that's going to move you.

As we begin, I want to put the following challenge in front of you:

AHAB.

If you saw that name and thought, *Oh, the captain forever chasing Moby Dick!*, you're right. But it's also an acronym for something that I have made a consistent habit in my life.

AHAB stands for Always Have a Book.

If I'm waiting for the kids to finish soccer practice, I have a book. If I'm sitting at an airport, I have a book. If I'm at a restaurant early for my reservation for a business lunch, I have a book. I discovered this practice when I asked that golden question of how successful people read: They always have a book at the ready.

I've got piles of books at my house, several tucked into my backpack, a few more in my gym bag. Wherever I go, I've got a book ready to go with me.

Here's something important for you to take note of. When I say *book*, for me, that's a physical book. I have found great value in holding a book in my hands, going through the steps I'll be explaining next, being able to quickly flip back and forth to the ideas and content that speak to my goals and my vision. However, I understand other people digest content more effectively through audiobooks, podcasts, and other nonprint means. Still others like to read visually but prefer digital or e-book formats on a device. If you tend to be an audiobook or device book reader, your path to AHAB is even simpler. As long as you've got your device with you, you can always have a book with you.

FROM DRIFT TO DRIVE

It's important to understand how you learn best, because it will make your reading experience more successful and enjoyable when you spend the bulk of your content consumption time in your chosen format. That said, I do want to encourage you, even if you typically like audio or digital content over physical books, to sprinkle some physical books into your book diet.

Make it a habit to fill those small gaps in your day with content that teaches you and inspires you, when you're running errands, getting your children to their activities, or waiting for your dentist. AHAB is one of your best strategies for leveraging time you already have toward your growth.

How to Crush a Book

A few years ago, I was thrilled to have lunch with Peter Daniels, the Australian billionaire speaker, author, and all-around amazing human. On all sides of me around that lunch table were incredible people, and you better believe we had our pens and paper out for a question-and-answer session with Mr. Daniels. People asked about business protocols, decision-making, and other fascinating topics.

And then it was my turn to voice a question.

"Mr. Daniels," I asked, "if there's one thing I could do that would make the greatest impact in my life, what would that be?"

Without skipping a beat, he smiled and responded, "Read."

Okay, short and sweet. But...

He graciously continued. "Chris, what happens when you begin to read is that you build in your mind a vocabulary, a vocabulary built on overcoming insurmountable odds. Your mind doesn't know the difference between what is real and what is not real. If you

STEP 3: FILTERING

can continue to put in your mind things that have already been done and what people have achieved, you can go farther."

He went on to share with me that when he was twenty-seven years old, he was an illiterate bricklayer. He was now in his seventies, both a well-read and widely-read billionaire with successful businesses, a happy family life, and a deep faith. He told me, "I've achieved over a billion dollars in success because of reading. I've read over five thousand books in my lifetime and I attribute the money I've made to that reading."

You better believe I started reading even more at that point. I took it far more seriously.

At first, I simply asked every successful person I met what they were reading. It was a great start. But over time, after buying more and more and more books, I found myself overwhelmed. I was spending a lot of time reading some books that I didn't quite relate to.

Then, I started to ask a question that shifted everything. Instead of only asking people what they read, I began asking successful people *how* they read.

That turned out to be a golden question. And the answers I discovered transformed reading for me. Those answers helped me form three information filters that are going to have you reading and absorbing and applying information in record time.

Successful people don't think about books and reading the way most everyone else does. They know that the information you're taking in needs to make its way through three specific types of filters: a content filter, a learning filter, and an action filter. That's how you crush a book, take the juice, and use what you've learned to propel you further.

95

FROM DRIFT TO DRIVE

The Content Filter

A friend of mine started a book club years ago. She and her friends would choose a book each month to read and then meet at one of the members' homes to discuss the plot, the writing style, what resonated with them in the book, and what they might have changed.

At one of the meetings, my friend was sharing how the mystery book selection for the month had kept her reading into the wee hours of the morning. "That book should come with a warning!" she exclaimed. "I had a busy day the next day but I absolutely could not put the book down until I knew who the culprit was!"

And then she heard something that absolutely shocked her.

"Oh," one of the book club members casually revealed, "I just go ahead and read the last few pages of the book ahead of time. That way, I don't have to stay up all night or get anxious about the outcome of the book. I already know the end."

My friend was completely flabbergasted! This sounded like a serious violation of book rules. Don't you always have to go through a book, page by page, until you reach the end? Don't you have to read the whole thing, even if it gets a little boring or isn't speaking to you anymore? You can't just skip to the good parts all willy-nilly, right?

Right?

Um, I'm gonna say *wrong*. I'm granting you permission, right now, today, to rethink how you move through a book.

This was part of my problem, once I fully aligned with the importance of books and reading in my life. As I shared with you earlier, I started to become overwhelmed with all the great books that were recommended to me. Over time I began to realize the following:

STEP 3: FILTERING

1. I was reading books that weren't applicable to me.

2. I was allowing material that had a "shiny object" factor to distract me.

3. I thought for some reason it didn't "count" unless I read a book cover to cover.

To make the most of my reading time, I needed a filter in place. Content Filters allow you to harvest more quickly what you need so you can leave the rest.

Filters are critical to this onboarding process of resources. As I like to tell the audiences I speak to, filtering fosters your future. Why? Because as you filter the information you're taking in, your decisions and your actions are being guided.

Let's break each of these down and install the content filter needed.

PROBLEM: I was reading books that weren't applicable to me.

SOLUTION: Test-drive.

Because I had newly arrived to understanding the importance of reading, I thought that each and every book recommended to me must be meant for me. That simply isn't true. Sometimes a book has been world changing for one person because its content is very specific to their situation and goals.

Today, I always take a book out for a test-drive, just like I do a new car I'm interested in. You've gone for a test-drive, right? You think through some basics: *Does it have enough seats for me and for my family? Does it have ample cargo space for groceries and luggage? Does it have features that are important to me, like a certain type of engine,*

FROM DRIFT TO DRIVE

leather upholstery, sound system? (And then, in my case, *Is the paint color one that will match one of my favorite outfits?* No judging, now. I'm just trying to be honest.)

On that test-drive, even if the engine is running fine, you still think about those features. After all, a car is a pricey investment, and you want to make sure it fits your needs and your season of life.

A book is the same way. It requires an investment of your time and attention, and you want to get the most out of that investment. When I test-drive a book, I look for the features I need for where I'm headed. If that book doesn't have them, I bless it and send it on its way.

Book summaries through a service like Blinkist are a great way to quickly test if a book speaks directly to your focus.[35] Platforms like Amazon often make a sample of the book available that includes the table of contents and a synopsis. For audiobooks, you are usually able to listen to the first five minutes before you buy, which includes the contents and the introduction. These elements allow you to test-drive the book and decide whether it's for you or not.

Look at the cover of a book you're considering and pay attention to the subtitle. What's the "pitch" of the book, the paragraph or two inside the front cover or in the description of the book online? Is it something you need?

You have to know what you need in order to succeed.

If you find it really difficult to determine if multiple books apply to you and your goals, I want to challenge you that you might still not have the clarity you need about where you want to go. I know that might be frustrating to hear, but I find it's true. When I'm not clear about my vision, it's hard to tell if something is going to

STEP 3: FILTERING

be of value to me. You must have clarity on what you're wanting to learn and why.

PROBLEM: I was allowing material that had a "shiny object" factor to distract me.

SOLUTION: Relentlessly focus.

Confession: I almost fell down the shiny object hole while researching this chapter. I was going to make a point about crows and how they collect shiny objects but it turns out there is a whole debate about whether crows actually are attracted to shiny objects and if it's a myth or established science and one source said that...

You get my point.

It can happen when you least expect it or for good reason (like my crow example), but the bottom line is that you must filter what is specific to your goal and stay on that track. Bust out a piece of paper and write your purpose at the top. Give it a good hard stare. Then take a glance at the book you've picked up or the tab you've opened or the podcast you've paused. Is the content related to your purpose? No? Then put it down. Close the tab. Exit the podcast. It doesn't need to go into the nest of information you're building, shiny or not.

PROBLEM: I thought for some reason it didn't "count" unless I read a book cover to cover.

SOLUTION: It always counts.

When you invest in learning, it always counts. When you apply something you've learned, it always counts. When you discover a sentence, a principle, an inspiration that carries you toward your

FROM DRIFT TO DRIVE

goal, even if you don't read or listen or watch the entirety of the source, it always counts.

Don't discount what counts.

The Learning Filter

Once you've filtered the content you're going to be reading, you'll now use what I call the Learning Filter. These are the methods I use for working through the chosen content and helping it stick in my brain. And here's some great news: When you use the techniques in the Learning Filter, you'll find that you're able to move through the content with greater efficiency and speed. As you get better and better at it, you'll be able to work through more and more material. And more material means more wisdom, insight, knowledge, and know-how for you.

Decide Ahead of Time

Ready to wildly increase the amount of helpful content you onboard? Stop reading *everything*.

Instead, *read what you need*.

One of my early problems in my reading and information onboarding journey was that I was reading entire books instead of looking for the content in those books that was most important to my goals. Talk about a great way to feel completely overwhelmed by your content pile! But once I started asking top leaders *how* they read, I discovered that they didn't feel confined to going through a book cover to cover. And so I decided I didn't have to be either.

Here's exactly how I work through a book.

STEP 3: FILTERING

First, I look at the front and back cover, the interior flaps, and the table of contents. While I've looked at these elements during my purchasing process, I'm now moving to working through the totality of the content. I really take a moment to consider the title, the subtitle, the copy on the cover, the chapter titles. After that short tour, I prime my mind. I ask myself, *What do I want to learn from this material?* I create a purpose for engaging with the book. When you decide what you want to learn, you're now programming your subconscious mind to know what to go look for.

Next, I open the book. I read the section titles, the bullet points, the featured quotes, the irregular text, the graphs. I do go through a page at a time, but I'm moving fast, only taking in those things that are designed to stand out.

Then, I put the book down.

Seriously. Put that book down. This is the point where I ask myself, *If I had to teach this tomorrow based on what I know so far, what would I teach?* Again, this is a tool for priming your mind.

Now, it's time for the second read-through. Yep, I'm reading it again.

This time I'm going through the book with my highlighter. I'm still looking for titles, bullet points, quotes, and irregular text. But this time I highlight those areas that really stand out to me. When something captures my attention enough that I'm highlighting it, that's my signal to go a little farther. I read the next few paragraphs that follow what I've highlighted.

As I'm moving through the material this second time, I keep the concept of what I would teach from it in mind. It keeps my brain in a posture of efficiently searching for the treasure and discarding

FROM DRIFT TO DRIVE

the rest. Depending on my goals, I might make a third and a fourth pass through the material. Overall, this process takes me about an hour, and at the conclusion of that time, I truly can get onstage or in an online presentation and teach what I've learned.

Read Faster

Like I've shared, I definitely was a fast driver back in my high school years.

Reading, on the other hand? It was a slog. I don't doubt that my slow reading speed was one of the reasons I thought I hated reading. It just took soooooo long. When I began to ask top leaders how they read, speed-reading came up again and again. I knew that if I wanted to become a lifelong reader and learner, I was going to have to make some changes to my reading speed.

I don't have any kind of marketing agreement or anything like that with the programs and teachers I'm going to mention throughout this chapter. These resources just work either for me or for others I've coached, helping increase reading speed.

I began to increase my reading speed through a program called Infinitemind.io.[36] It's an online program with an inexpensive monthly subscription that helps train your brain to read 50 percent faster. It gives you exercises to strengthen your eyes, because your eyes are like a muscle and they have to be built up. In order to read faster, you have to train.

Infinitemind.io is not the only course or method out there. I have many friends who have found great success with the Evelyn Wood speed-reading courses and books.[37] You can also check out Dr. Paul Scheele's PhotoReading techniques.[38] The point is to train

STEP 3: FILTERING

your mind to read faster, utilizing a speed-reading method that works for you.

You may be thinking, *But Chris, I'm an audiobook kind of a person*. I've got great news. There is a little feature on your listening device that will allow you to increase the playing speed to 1.5x or 2x the normal speed or even faster. Sure, the narrator is going to sound like a chipmunk, but the novelty of that might even keep your attention a little better. Ready for more great news? The average brain can process just fine up to 400 words per minute.[39] I'm confident you can handle at least 500. And there is more and more research indicating that we can process up to 800 words a minute by training and intentionally listening to material.[40]

Whether you're a physical-book fan or an audiobook reader, the bottom line is you can speed up the process effectively.

Train For It

Of course I want you reading more and more material, and I want you reading it faster and faster. But one of the top questions I'm asked when I teach this method, which I call Crush a Book, is about retention. After all, if you can't retain what you're reading, what's the point?

This is where I make good on a promise from the previous chapter, when I told you I would be sharing a life-changing seven-minute video I watched on YouTube. In the middle of my pursuit to become a more effective and prolific reader, I discovered a video called "Mind Mapping by Stephen Pierce" on Pierce's YouTube channel @impulsiveprofits.[41] It was my introduction to how to be more intentional about retaining the information I was taking in.

FROM DRIFT TO DRIVE

I decided to test-drive it at church one Sunday. After the service, Jenee asked me what I thought of the sermon. I was able to reconstruct for her the entire sermon outline, important takeaways, key stories, and more.

"How did you do that?" she gasped. After all, we'd been married long enough for her to know that I could get distracted while taking out the trash. I shared with her the mind mapping techniques I learned from that video. Mind mapping has been a key part of my process ever since.

Mind mapping is a way of visually organizing the material you're taking in through making "maps" of the information. Research shows that those who mind map the content they are interacting with show a significant increase in retention over those who only read the text.[42] Mind mapping also increases your critical thinking skills and innovation.[43] You can use mind mapping for both written and audio material.

Just like speed-reading techniques, you need to learn which method of mind mapping works best for you. For me, the principles in Stephen Pierce's video, along with other teachings on mind mapping, helped me develop a process for myself. I always have my highlighter with me as I'm working through a book and then use my iPad for mind mapping, to jot down the key words, chapter concepts, important facts, and more as I work through each chapter. I also use a program on my iPad called iThoughts[44] that allows me to map how I'm engaging with the material. The beauty of mapping this way is that it not only wildly increases my retention but also gives me a powerful graphic that I can share with my team about what I've learned. I created a mind map for writing this book, and I

STEP 3: FILTERING

have mind maps of the content I consume. I can go back at any time to revisit material. And because I can "see" in my mind's eye how I mapped things out, I have a path for easily going into my mind and finding the information I need, when I need it.

* * *

Let's pause and recap the top ways to Crush a Book we've learned so far using the Content and Learning Filters:

1. **AHAB**: Always Have a Book

2. **Test-drive**: Does this book or content meet your focus and purpose?

3. **Relentlessly Focus**: Don't get distracted by shiny objects.

4. **It Always Counts**: What counts is not in "finishing" the book cover to cover but in harvesting what you need.

5. **Decide Ahead of Time**: Filter a book's content by first reading the cover material, tables of contents, quotes, irregular text, and other visual markers. Make a second pass through the book highlighting what stands out, reading through the paragraphs that follow. Ask yourself how you would teach the material.

6. **Read Faster**: Build your visual and mental muscle for moving through material quickly.

7. **Train For It**: Use mind mapping to create retention and recall for the material you consume.

And now it's time to discover the third technique to Crush a Book, the Action Filter.

FROM DRIFT TO DRIVE

The Action Filter

After you've worked through the preliminary information you've gathered and filtered, what's next? Was this all just for the purpose of being able to spout leadership and personal growth trivia at your next cohort meeting? (*He's got jokes!*) Obviously not. You've put effort and time and investment into moving through material. Now it's time to take action on what you've learned.

But what action? What are the next steps? It can feel confusing, trying to figure out what to do with the information you've onboarded. This is where I sometimes see people lapse into complacency again or slip into that shiny object mentality that always seems to come for us. It's all too easy to confuse this absorption of information with action. While really soaking up good information is a critical part of your journey, if that information stays locked in a tidy file cabinet in your mind and that's all you ever do with it, all that onboarding has been for nothing.

That's why it's so important for you to move on to what I call the Action Filter.

Throw a pebble into a group of high-capacity, low-complacency leaders, and you're going to hit the latest technology and gadgets and apps time and again. I like all the productivity gizmos and have certainly taken a bunch of them out for a spin. There's something inspiring about trying out a new platform or approach when it comes to getting intentional on making good on your steps to your goals.

But if you think that's the direction we're headed in this next filter, then I've got some news. To utilize this next filter, you can leave the technology and the widgets behind. The Action Filter requires one of the simplest sets of office tools out there. But don't be fooled

STEP 3: FILTERING

by its simplicity. I can promise you, it's something that has made all the difference in me taking the next right steps toward my goals.

Are you ready to go shopping? Here's what you need to live your dreams, bust through your complacency, soar to new heights, and charge the hill.

- A pack of 4x6 index cards
- A pen

Ta-da! Wild stuff, I know. But I want you to grab an index card from the stack, pick up that pen, and write the numbers 1–5 down the left-hand side of the card.

Here's where the magic comes in. These are the five questions I want you to ask yourself.

1. What do I need to read today?

2. What do I need to listen to today?

3. Who do I need to call today?

4. What do I need to do today?

5. What am I looking for today?

Now write down an answer to each question next to the corresponding number on the card.

Over and over again, people talk to me about their to-do lists. They've got a million things on those lists that they are trying to plow through, everything from getting a quote on a new roof for their house to putting their client list into a better CRM. Great. It's not a bad idea to have an inventory of the tasks to be done. What a standard to-do list can't do, however, is make the priorities the priorities. I can tell you, for sure, that tasks will always try to hijack your day.

FROM DRIFT TO DRIVE

That is the beauty of this 4x6 Action Filter. Notice the last word of each question: *today*. Every single day, you must ask yourself if the activities you have laid out are the next steps to take to get you closer to the goal you've set for yourself. Someone may have handed off a great book to you that they enjoyed on a recent vacation. Is it what you need to read *today*? There's the interesting true crime podcast your neighbor told you about. Do you really need to listen to it *today*? When I was building my coaching business, I was looking for new clients *today*. When I was building my speaking business, I was looking for speaking opportunities *today*, not half an hour of TikTok dances.

Complacency can be a shape-shifter. It can show up in a variety of ways in your life. One of the ways I often see it show up is in the form of a to-do list, a way of making you feel like you're being productive and busy without actually making any progress. The only way to conquer this form of complacency is to be highly intentional with each line on that index card, to truly filter the actions we're taking with the time we have in an allotted twenty-four-hour period.

I'd been working with a real go-getter of a young guy, someone who was making great progress toward his goals. He reached out one day, asking if we could have a quick call, that he had something he could really use some help with. We jumped on the phone.

"Chris," he told me, his voice excited, tinged with nerves, "I have an incredible opportunity in front of me."

"Great," I responded. "Tell me about it."

He started talking even faster. "It's a fire deal on a five-bedroom house with a boat dock on a lake! I know it won't last long and I…" He stopped to take a quick breath, so I injected an important question into the split-second pause.

STEP 3: FILTERING

"Were you looking for a house *today*?"

"Um…well, no, but Chris, this is just really an awesome deal! I don't know if I could pass up the opportunity!"

So I helped him run it through the Action Filter. "Let me ask you this, if you were looking for a house today, would it be a five-bedroom house on the lake?"

"Not necessarily…" he confessed.

"And would you be looking for a house with a boat dock?"

"No…"

"And are you looking to buy a boat for the boat dock that goes with the five-bedroom house?"

The light dawned. "No. Thanks, Chris!" And he hung up the phone, clarity restored, the Action Filter bringing order back to his priorities.

Could that house have been a great opportunity? Sure. Would it also have been a potential massive distraction from what he had established as his primary heading? Absolutely.

The Action Filter is critical as you take all the great ideas and information and start putting it into practice. The Action Filter clears out the shiny stuff, makes decisions easier, keeps the learning process as a priority, and keeps what's essential in your view.

One simple index card. Five simple questions.

Massive impact toward your future.

Filter your actions and watch your focus sharpen to what is most powerful and most essential.

* * *

FROM DRIFT TO DRIVE

As you put the Content, Learning, and Action Filters into place, you're going to experience something amazing. I know all that content you're working through can feel like a surging river of material, swirling and cluttered with both treasure and debris. But just like the purest drinking water, when you allow it to move through a series of filters, what you're left with is the most hydrating stuff, the liquid gold that takes you farther into the horizon of your dreams.

As you get better and better with these filters, you'll be able to move more and more quickly, with confidence and decisiveness. You'll have the wind of the wisdom of a thousand experts at your back, the clear beacon of your goal in your sights, and the clear next steps that will make up your day-to-day. Read what you need, take what serves your goal, curate your day with a simple index card. There is magic in Filtering and it's yours for the journey.

STEP 4: GUIDANCE
The Bridge to Experience and Wisdom

You've read yourself a good stack of books. You're getting your reading pace up to speed. You're retaining more, immersing yourself in the language and skills and ideas that will bring you closer to making your aim a reality.

This is the point in the journey where I see some people want to skip way ahead. A couple of podcasts, a good TED Talk, and two or three books into a how-to toward their goal, and they're ready to hang out their shingles as some kind of new expert.

I'm all for getting into action mode quickly, trying things out

FROM DRIFT TO DRIVE

and making adjustments. But I'm so sold on the step we're going to explore in this chapter (and also the step that follows) that I want you to take a breath for me and really settle in.

You can get all kinds of book knowledge, and you should. But I want you to be able to accelerate the impact of that information you've been taking in. And to do that, you need some time in the real world of what you want to do.

You need a guide to take you along the trail.

Trail Angels

His name is Kami Rita. He's in his mid-fifties and he has done something that no one else on the planet has ever done. Frankly, it wouldn't surprise me if no one can ever again achieve what he has. He's done it without any of the advantages you might expect. He's not had formal education. He doesn't have top nutritionists and sports physiotherapists on hand to get him primed. But make no mistake, he's accomplished what could arguably be seen as the most impressive achievement of physical endurance and performance ever known to humankind.

Kami Rita has summited Everest thirty times as a Sherpa, as a guide.[45] I have to say that again. Thirty. Times. (And, by the way, when he submitted for the thirtieth time, it was his second ascent in ten days; as in, he'd hit his twenty-ninth ascent just a week and a half before.) The mountain that routinely kills an average of over four people a year, the mountain that has defeated so many who have tried to scale its heights, Kami Rita has made his average day at work.

And you likely have never heard of him.

Kami Rita has worked as a Sherpa in the Himalayas since the

STEP 4: GUIDANCE

mid-1990s. And you better believe that were I ever to decide I wanted to climb Everest, Kami Rita is the guy I'd want to learn from, the trail angel who has the experience and record I'd want as a guide. I could watch all the documentaries about Everest. I could fill my brain with the details about the first base camp and the second and the North Col and all the other alpinist details. It would be important background work to center my mind and learn the language and set my sites. But think about what it would be like to distill all the information and then get to learn from the best of the best. Kami Rita would be *the* guy, and getting guidance from someone like him would clearly accelerate my understanding and ascent, were Everest ever to be my goal.

We need trail angels, you and me. People who have been where we want to go. People who have tried and failed and gotten back up and succeeded. People who have gathered real-time experience and have it to share. Some things you need to know are going to be taught. Other things are going to be *caught*. There's nothing like getting to watch someone do what they do. There's tremendous insight in taking what you've learned through the Gathering and Filtering processes and then observing someone who has successfully put many of those factors into action. As we've talked about, each step is mission critical. And each one has a uniquely potent contribution to your progress.

That's why the fourth step, Guidance, is so important.

In earlier centuries in this country, becoming an apprentice was an important rite of passage if someone wanted to make their living at a certain skill. If you wanted to be a blacksmith, you'd work with a seasoned blacksmith to learn. If you wanted to be a pastry chef

FROM DRIFT TO DRIVE

or a painter or a sculptor, you'd work for and in close proximity to a true craftsman.

Somewhere along the way, we seem to have lost the art of apprenticing. Sure, you might have been an intern for a few weeks one summer during college. But typically we've reduced our understanding of interning or apprenticeship as something of a test-drive for a possible career, deciding, say, if we really want to go on to veterinary school when we complete our undergraduate degree in the next year or two.

When I talk about Guidance, I'm talking about a type of apprenticing that's very different.

You already have clarity on what you want. You've decided to truly focus and go for it in this fresh chapter of your life. You're committed to shaking off complacency and reaching for your next adventure. What you need now is proximity, to be adjacent to those who have gone where you want to go.

According to a 2024 article on mentoring statistics, 76 percent of people said that they think mentoring is important to their growth, but only 37 percent had established guidance relationships. And check this out: 97 percent of those who have a mentor said that it has been powerful and valuable.[46] When I look at that math, it shows me just how important it is to get intentional about getting the guidance you need to go where you want to go.

When I use the word *guidance* to describe this step in the framework, I do so with intentionality. I could have used *mentoring* to describe this step, and I think it's a good word. I'll use it interchangeably with guidance throughout this chapter. But I want you to think of guidance, to think of mentoring, in a fresh way. However

STEP 4: GUIDANCE

you might have thought of it in the past, I'd ask you to *let that go*. You're going to be looking for a specific *type* of guidance. Getting to where you want to go is easier when you have someone to follow. When you seek guidance and mentorship, you're crossing the bridge that connects experience and wisdom.

Front of the Line

How do you go about finding the right kind of guidance?

It's a great question. At first blush, you might want to be mentored by whoever seems to be the top name or has the biggest platform in the arena in which you want to play. I understand that. I'm asking you to dream big when it comes to ditching complacency and getting excited about realizing another layer of your potential. So why wouldn't you think about the biggest names in your industry or interests?

However, who you choose as a mentor holds an exceptionally powerful place in your life. Mentors mold maturity. When you think about the goals you set for yourself in the first step of Clarity, what kind of person do you want to be when you get to where you're going? After all, there are people who have accomplished what you say you want to accomplish. But have they accomplished these things with the same kind of morals and values you hold dear?

People can get stuck right at the starting line when it comes to finding guidance, finding a mentor. Over the years, I've developed a simple two-part recipe that will help you get the guidance and support you need. Before I share it, though, I want you to spend a little time considering the following questions.

FROM DRIFT TO DRIVE

Do you have clarity on what you want to learn?
Because you've already committed to a destination you're driving toward, because you've already started gathering and onboarding the information you need for that heading, you likely are beginning to know what you don't know. In considering someone for mentorship, jot down three to five of those not-yet-knowns that you want to learn from them.

Let's say you have a goal of becoming a personal development coach. You've been reading and learning about the industry. Perhaps what you want to learn specifically from someone is how they developed their client base, how they scheduled their days, and how they put together their packages. Coming under someone's guidance can help you learn specifically how they accomplished those things.

If you're struggling to identify what you would want to learn in a guidance relationship, I suspect you still lack the clarity you need on where you actually want to go. When you have clarity on your goal, important questions will emerge specific to how someone has accomplished the same goal. The type of guidance I'm talking about here is for when you have clarity on your mission. If you're still trying to figure out what you want to do, I'd encourage you to go back to Steps 1 and 2 and spend more time getting focused. A potential mentor needs to be able to help guide you in a definitive way, not in a smattering of half-baked aspirations. If you're still trying to get clarity, you're not yet ready for this type of guidance.

Who is known for what you want to learn?
There may be people you admire, people who seem to have success in a different or adjacent field. You might be tempted to search them

STEP 4: GUIDANCE

out for guidance. I'd encourage you at this point to resist that temptation. It's not that they might not have some helpful general ideas for you. But, remember, you've got a specific horizon line you're heading toward, and that means you need a particular set of information. If your goal is to become a fantastic photographer for, say, luxury performance vehicles, you don't really need to be mentored by someone who does maternity and newborn portraiture, right? You're looking for the people who do what you want to do and who know what you need to know.

Does this person resonate with you, communicate in the way in which you learn?

You've got a unique way of learning and receiving information, genuine to you. Sometimes, there can be a great teacher out there, one whose guidance helps a lot of people. But if their way of teaching and guiding simply doesn't connect with you, the majority of what you're likely to absorb is frustration.

Do they share your values?

If someone has built a business, launched a podcast, or started an initiative but they've done it by ignoring their family, compromising their most important relationships, or through using people, is that really who you want to learn from? Sure, theirs might be *one* way in which that kind of success is built. But *it's not the only way*. There are other people who can provide guidance to you who value their relationships and who don't use anxiety and stress as their fuel. Find guidance from those you align with, not from those who cross the line.

FROM DRIFT TO DRIVE

Do they have the results you want?

Let's say you'd like to start a real estate business as your next venture. You think about someone selling property in your region who seems to be doing well. Her face is on billboards. You've been to her website and it's pretty spiffy. She shows up in the Lifestyles section of the local paper at various events.

That's all great.

But does she actually sell houses, sell property, at the volume and level to which you aspire? There can be a big gap between what someone presents as their level of expertise and what their actual results are. Sometimes the marketing matches the reality and sometimes it doesn't. Dig a little deeper to make sure that the person you seek out for learning actually knows how to get where you want to go. Verify if their results are hype or true-fruit ripe.

The Guidance Two-Part Recipe

This Guidance step is sometimes misunderstood or misused. But when you fully appreciate and make guidance part of your growth practice, you'll discover doors opening and opportunities showing up that wouldn't have otherwise.

As my sales and coaching business grew, a new goal emerged for me.

I wanted to be a speaker.

I wanted to help people by sharing the things I had learned in my journey for growth and leadership. I wanted to teach. I wanted to equip more people to go farther in their dreams.

The only problem was I had no idea how to be a public speaker, how to launch myself into that world, and what it would take to get

STEP 4: GUIDANCE

there. I needed some people to guide me, but how do you get a busy and successful speaker to agree to mentor you?

I have a two-part recipe for that.

Part One: Seek to Serve

"Can you run a video camera?"

I hesitated a split second. *I mean, how hard could it be, right?*

"I'd be happy to," I responded.

And just like that, I was the lead videographer for a noted speaker in St. Louis. I spent the day behind a camera, capturing the onstage sessions for this speaker while she presented to a large and engaged audience.

Was I some kind of skilled cinematographer, using all the lingo and capturing unique shots? No. But I *was* someone who was willing to serve and to help. And even though sitting behind the camera wasn't my end goal, I had a feeling that serving in that way might just help me get to where I wanted to head next.

Like I said, I wanted to become a speaker. I'd followed the first three steps: developed clarity for that goal, gathered resources, filtered those resources. From engaging those steps, I had a pretty good idea of the general contours of important skills for a speaker to have, and I'd picked up some tips for having a speaking business. But I knew there were some things I needed to learn by getting guidance, receiving mentoring from someone who was doing what I wanted to do. And I didn't have the money at the time to pay someone to help me.

So I began by thinking about who in my community was known for public speaking, people who were getting on stages that

FROM DRIFT TO DRIVE

I would like to be on one day. I did a Google search for speakers in the area, looking at their messaging, values, and results. I picked up the phone and started calling them, one by one. I'd say, "Hey! I want to start a speaking business too! Can I buy you a cheap cup of coffee and pick your brain for all the information, techniques, and ideas you've gathered with blood, sweat, and tears over the last couple of decades? And could you hold me accountable? And could you connect me to your network?"

Gotcha. Sounds foolproof, right?

No, that is absolutely *not* what I did. And that's not what I want you to do when it comes to practicing this step of Guidance.

Let's start over. What I did say was this:

"Hello. My name's Chris Robinson. I'd love to find out more about professional speaking. If there's any way that I can *volunteer* for you, please let me know." Dial, rinse, repeat.

One of the speakers I called, Lethia Owens, said, "That's very nice of you. I don't have anything now, but if something comes up, I'll call you."

I didn't hear from her for a few days. But before the week was out, she actually did call me back. "Hey, Chris, my cameraman canceled for a speaking job I have tomorrow. Would you be my cameraman for this event?"

I told her I would. The next day, I drove to downtown St. Louis and served as her cameraman.

Purely with the motive of serving.

Mouth closed.

Expectations absent.

Ears and heart open.

STEP 4: GUIDANCE

As I mentioned, there was nothing to brag about in my camera skills. I'm sure I provided pretty bad footage with the way I jerked the camera around. But, hey, I was *free*!

During that day, at her invitation, we grabbed lunch together. Over sandwiches, Lethia said, "I know you wanted to find out more about speaking. Can I answer any questions for you?"

I was prepared with a list of questions that I wanted to ask people who had been able to build a successful speaking business. While I certainly had not shown up to volunteer with an expectation that Lethia "owed" me answers, I was ready for the opportunity if it came. I presented my questions and Lethia graciously answered in the time she had available. Then, it was time for her to get back to speaking at her next session, and I had videography to do.

At the end of the day, Lethia sought me out and asked if I would be able to come to the next day's conference sessions. I told her I'd be happy to serve again.

The following day, I set up the camera, shot Lethia's morning sessions, and was delighted when we got to have lunch again. She once again asked if I had questions and shared with me her experiences. As lunch was wrapping up and I got ready to return to the camera, Lethia had a question for me.

"You've been in all my sessions and you've seen the material I'm presenting. I'd like to have you speak onstage today, to have that opportunity. I'd like for you to take one of the slides from my presentation from yesterday and speak on it. Do you think you could present for about five minutes or so on one of the slides?"

Wow, this was unexpected! "Absolutely," I said.

FROM DRIFT TO DRIVE

My five-minute session went well. And from there, Lethia became a mentor in my life. She provided important guidance and wisdom as I began my speaking career. And it started because I genuinely looked for a way to serve someone in the field I was interested in.

When I was sharing this principle of serving with a friend, they asked me how it would translate in the corporate working environment. If you're working in a business and want to learn about getting to the next level in the organization, borrow this page from my time of working in sales. I went to my boss and asked him, "What are your least favorite job responsibilities?" He laid out for me three or four things that he really didn't like doing. I told him that I would be happy to take on those things for him, in addition to the defined workload of my current position. Doing so gave me greater proximity to him as we interacted on these items. And when the day came that he moved another rung up the ladder, I was the obvious candidate to replace him, since I was the person who had actual experience with several of the responsibilities of that role.

No matter what you're aiming for, no matter the environment, whether you're volunteering for someone or looking for people to provide you guidance within an organization, when you offer to serve, when you come alongside and help from an unselfish heart, you'll be amazed at what you learn. Proximity, over time, opens doors. When you show up with a heart to truly serve, you've put yourself in a good spot for when a door of opportunity opens.

Part Two: Pay-to-Play

The first person you're going to seek guidance from is someone you connect with in your community or workplace, someone you can

STEP 4: GUIDANCE

serve on a consistent basis and observe how they achieve at the level to which you aspire. Then there's a second person I want you to seek guidance from. And this one is going to require you to put your wallet where your dreams are.

There are professional coaches, consultants, and conferences that can provide incredible guidance for your next steps, that can give you the feedback and direction you need to get you to where you want to go. This will likely mean a financial investment on your part. Because you will be putting money on the table, you should have some solid expectations about what you want to gain from this expertise.

Sometimes I hear pushback from folks who don't like the idea of paying a coach. They say they're serious about taking their ideas and vision to the next level, but they struggle to level up when it comes to the caliber of people they need to bring to the table to learn from. They resist investing in going to the conference. They don't want to put money down in order to get the coach they need to truly go pro.

For example, say you want to write a book. And let's say you devote some time over several months writing up early chapters, getting your ideas down on paper. You say you're serious about getting a book out there, so you ask your friends, you ask some work colleagues, "Hey, who do you know who works in publishing and writing?" You get the name of someone and reach out, asking them to read over what you've written and to give you feedback. You also ask if they could give you a call so you can ask them all about publishing and receive all kinds of tips and ideas. And you expect them to do this out of the goodness of their heart, even though this is their profession, a profession that's taken them years of experience to build.

123

FROM DRIFT TO DRIVE

Now, hold on. You wouldn't just walk into a doctor's office and expect him to, out of the goodness of his heart, give you a diagnosis. You wouldn't expect an attorney to draw up legal papers for you just out of a sense of altruism. You'd expect to pay professionals in their fields to handle such important matters.

In the same vein, when you approach the professionals you need to help you in your next steps, expect to pay professional prices for those services. If it's a book, hire the book coach. If it's to become a leader in your organization, hire the leadership trainer. If it's to successfully switch industries or start a completely new business, hire the business coach. Get to the conference. Get in the room with the people who are pulling oars in the direction you want to go. Yes, asking your sister-in-law to read your book or asking your friend at church to look at your business plan can be "free," and I'm sure they're lovely people who want the best for you. But in only seeking input from those who don't have the experience and expertise for where you want to go, you're engaging in yet another form of complacency. You're playing small, you're hedging the bet, and it will show as you try to move forward.

Pay-to-Play is also about learning from a distance. If you can't get to the conference in person, look for online options. Join the group that meets on Zoom with the expert to boost your business and your goals. You might not get individualized attention or the closest access, but you're still learning. You still have access to that person's experience. I've already mentioned that my experience with John Maxwell and his leadership and personal development wisdom started in the basement of a church, watching videos. As I set new and bigger goals for myself, I made further investments in his guidance. I paid to attend

STEP 4: GUIDANCE

a conference. Then I invested in closer access through group coaching.

When I added pay-to-play to the seek-to-serve guidance I was getting from people like Lethia, it wasn't like I was flush with cash. It was a choice to invest in myself and in my goals. I did that by becoming part of the John Maxwell Team, paying to be part of the program.

* * *

You've likely noticed that I've used the word *proximity* frequently throughout this chapter. It comes from an old French word and means "nearness in place, time, or relation."[47] When I invested in John Maxwell trainings, it gave me proximity to John. It didn't give me a right to take away from John's time, but it meant that I had a shared experience, being in the same venue, hearing John's teachings, seeing how he carried himself, how he treated others in the room.

In guidance, whether seeking to serve or paying to play, you'll have proximity in at least one of the three categories of proximity: place, time, and relation.

A Couple of Warnings and a Bucket of Rewards

There's a debate happening, literally at the highest point on Earth. Each year, about 800 people attempt to summit Mount Everest. Some have put in the training and work as best they can before they arrive. Some have not. Some make it to the top and others don't. In 2023, 667 people successfully summitted. And eighteen people died.[48]

The debate comes because a lot of people who say they want to "climb" Everest are depending on Sherpas to literally drag them up the mountain. It costs between $65,000 and $125,000 to try

FROM DRIFT TO DRIVE

to summit Everest.[49] For some of the people who head out for this adventure, that's as much investment as they put into it, paying their fee and figuring that the Sherpa who comes as part of the adventure package will do the rest.

When those hikers hit the trail, having not done the physical training truly needed for the intense conditions and the high elevation, their presence on the route is at best a traffic jam and irritant to better-conditioned climbers and their guides, and at worst it creates even more treacherous situations in an already extremely dangerous environment.

When I look at the accounts of Sherpas, hikers, the body count, and all the rest, I can see clearly at issue a misunderstanding about what guidance—what mentoring—truly means. I think about Kami Rita, who we talked about at the top of the chapter, and how it would be so easy to miss his expertise in an expectation that he should just drag you up the mountain instead of learning from him how it can be climbed.

It's been my observation through the years that a lot of people understand that they need mentoring. But what do they seem to expect from finding a mentor; what do they want to receive from a mentor? That's where I see a problem. For whatever reason, we've somehow transposed our understanding of mentoring to mean that we want someone to get us across the line. Someone to hold us accountable to our goals. Someone to call in favors and get us in the rooms we want to be in and propel our potential forward for us.

That's not guidance, friend. That's not mentoring.

Here's how it should work: We learn from them—and then we do the work.

126

STEP 4: GUIDANCE

We also sometimes confuse coaching and consulting toward a goal with counseling and therapy. My colleague Valorie Burton gives a lot of great insights in her teachings on keeping the lanes between coaching and counseling clear.[50] Coaching, guidance, mentoring is for helping you move more quickly toward your goals, helping you overcome obstacles that pop up in that endeavor, and for giving you ideas and direction for moving forward.

Counseling, on the other hand, is for when you have open wounds in your life that are holding you back. For when you don't know what you want. For when you need healing to start to dream again.

I think it's one of the bigger mistakes I see people make when seeking out mentoring, when investing in conferences and coaching. They're expecting those avenues of guidance to patch over what needs to be cleaned out and healed. They're expecting someone to establish that first step of Clarity for them, instead of discovering how to take that step of Clarity and place it as a guiding star.

You have the responsibility to climb your own mountain of potential. There are also a wealth of people who you can watch and from whom you can learn. But their job is not to bodily carry you to where you want to go. I want you to hit the summit knowing that *you* did it.

The tool kit for getting all the juice from guidance?

1. **Walk in humbleness.** Remember, the right mentor wants to see you succeed. They're sharing what they're sharing to help you get where you want to go.

2. **Be open.** Your mentor will likely have ideas and feedback for you. Your openness to receiving that feedback can be the very key to unlocking your next level.

FROM DRIFT TO DRIVE

3. **Exhibit initiative.** Show up early, show up excited, show up ready to learn and to serve.

4. **Be confident.** Know that you're on a good heading and that you can achieve what you've put your mind to. Have faith in your mentor's abilities and the techniques and strategies they've used to achieve what they have.

5. **Show respect.** Remember, your mentor is not your peer. They're a rank or more above your current post. While you share the same value as human beings, they have seniority. Use your manners; honor their experience and wisdom.

6. **Speak your gratitude.** Thank people who invest in you, who allow you to look behind the curtain of their success.

Guidance has two parts:

Serving.

And...

Investing.

And when you're committed to that, it will fuel everything that comes next. There's a bucket of rewards that come when you're committed to serving someone who is guiding you and when you invest in the coaching and services that equip you well. A faster climb. A more efficient path. A benefit of combined wisdom.

I'm confident, too, that when you reach the summit of your vision, you'll have the opportunity in turn to serve as a guide to those starting on a similar path. That's the way of becoming a trail angel, learning from others, navigating the switchbacks and rock faces to make your way, and then sharing what you've learned with those excited and eager to hear.

STEP 5:
RELATIONSHIPS
The Right Rooms

There was some kind applause and some pats on the back as I wrapped up my presentation. I'd shared my business plan for building my speaking business with the networking group I was part of. I showed them a couple of business funnels I was working on. It was a lovely group of people, always kind and supportive of each other, but, I have to say, it was pretty quiet when I wrapped up that day. Nobody had any input.

After the meeting, I headed out to the parking lot, walking with one of my closest friends, Jason. "That was kind of weird," I said. Frankly, I was a little upset, given how much time and thought I'd put into the presentation, how much it mattered to me to launch my speaking business. "Nobody had anything to say."

Jason sighed. "Chris, what you had to share was great. It's just

FROM DRIFT TO DRIVE

that no one in the room knows anyone who's done what you're trying to do." We walked a few more steps, and then he put his hand on my arm, stopping us mid–parking lot. "I think you're in the wrong room."

Jason was 100 percent right.

And if I'd continued to be part of that group, I could have lived and died in my cubicle at work.

Just like I pushed you in developing your vision, I'm going to push you with this next step: Relationships. This is a key area where I find complacency hides, tucked in the corners and secreted under the names of Kind and Supportive.

Hey, Chris, what on earth are you talking about? I need people on my side. One of my love languages is words of affirmation.

Believe me, there was a time that I would have been looking at my above statements on relationships and would have thought the very same thing. And I absolutely want people in my life who give me words of encouragement, just like you do. But I want you to do a deep dive into your own heart and into your goals and ask yourself a really tough question:

Am I in the wrong rooms?

I could have given the group I described an absolute A+ when it came to being affirming and supportive. But in the culture of that particular slice of community, there was no actionable feedback. Each time I would give a presentation, all I heard was that I'd done a nice job. That particular networking group didn't understand where I wanted to go, and I in turn was sort of dragging my feet about getting into a community of people who were looking higher and pushing harder.

STEP 5: RELATIONSHIPS

It was nice to be in the cushioned experience of my current group. It felt safe.

And a healthy community should feel safe. But it should also feel like a safe place to fail. A safe place to hear tough feedback. A safe place to try things and see how they land. My mistake was not in seeking out a community with kind individuals. It was in not seeking out a community of kind individuals who understood where I wanted to go and were willing to care about me enough to push me to get there, no excuses.

Maybe you've had an experience like I did with that initial networking group, where nothing was necessarily wrong, but there also wasn't a point of connection. Or, perhaps you've had an experience on the opposite end of the spectrum. You lay out your goal, you talk about what you're doing to get there, you open the door for feedback, and instead of getting a general *Nice job* kind of vanilla response, you instead get people throwing the equivalent of goal-busting tomatoes at you.

That will never work.

My neighbor tried to do something like that and he blew all his life savings.

These are phrases one might hear from others as advice:

- That will never work.
- I don't get what you are trying to do.
- Is this just your ego talking?

You can walk out of a session like that feeling as if you've got egg on your face and crazy in your heart. Those kinds of rooms can drain the air out of your tires and the purpose out of your resolve.

The Right Rooms

As a species, we humans struggle when it comes to new ideas, when it comes to trying a new way. Back around five hundred years ago, there was a man who walked into a variety of different rooms and explained a new concept. He had some great information and data behind what he was saying. He had clarity on his direction. But, whew, people didn't like it. His faith was questioned. His intelligence. He was accused of all manner of things, not least of which was that in promoting his new idea, he was diminishing and putting down all of humankind! He was definitely in the wrong rooms at times.

His name was Nicolaus Copernicus, and he was a mathematician, religious minister, and astronomer. When he presented his work that the sun in fact was the center of our universe and that Earth was revolving around it, the wrong people in the wrong rooms tried to make it sound like good ol' Nic was missing a few screws. Today, we can laugh about how wrong they all had it and how right he did, but imagine if Copernicus had let all those dissenting voices stop his research and calculations.

In the wrong rooms, Copernicus was seen as a madman and an apostate. In the right rooms, Copernicus was seen as a genius.[51]

So let's take a look at how to recognize whether we're in the right room.

The Right Rooms Have Bigger Windows

As I started to do more work with Maxwell Leadership, I received a unique opportunity to accompany John Maxwell to a fundraising gathering. I sat at a round table, covered in a crisp white cloth, with several interesting and impressive individuals. We all listened

STEP 5: RELATIONSHIPS

attentively as John spelled out the people we could help and the efforts we could supplement through this fundraising effort.

And then I got to see something I'd never seen before. Something that I don't think up to that point I would have even known was possible. The people I was sitting with started to talk among themselves at the conclusion of John's presentation, and they raised, just at our table, $500,000.

What?

I threw $500 into the collective pile to bring the total to $500,500. But that 500 bucks, while a chunk of serious change to my budget, paid off in vision I'd not had before. I was at a table where five other individuals, in just a couple minutes, each put $100,000 toward a cause they believed in.

My vision up to that point was to get a house big enough for my wife and kids (we had four at this point), to have a couple of nice cars, and to go on a couple of good vacations. But sitting in that room, at that table that day, changed me. It showed me that radical vision and radical growth could lead to radical generosity. It showed me that there were attainable levels out there that I hadn't really considered before. It showed me that, even though I had some wonderful relationships and community, I was playing too small.

While you might feel most comfortable in the rooms you've been in before, where you know the view, where you know the expectations, it's time to get into rooms that have bigger windows. What do I mean by that? I mean you want to surround yourself with people who can see farther, who have a view of a bigger picture than you're used to.

That's what I realized, sitting around the table with those big donors: They had a far wider perspective than I'd ever experienced.

FROM DRIFT TO DRIVE

They could look out the window, so to speak, and see possibilities, ideas, and fields of harvests that I had to squint to see. When I sat with people like them, opportunities I didn't even know were possible started to pop up on the radar.

The Right Rooms Have the Right Kind of Encouragement

"I hate being a lawyer."

I'd just met the guy, but I believed him.

I was in Indonesia on a speaking trip and had a few hours free one evening. I love listening to live music, so I got a recommendation for a restaurant close to my hotel that had a band. I was minding my own business, listening to some great music and relaxing, when this man approached me. He stated the obvious, that I didn't look like I was from around there, and asked me about myself. I shared that I had traveled to Indonesia from the States and that I was in his city for a speaking engagement. After I added a little bit about my work, he inquired, "Can I ask you something?"

I nodded.

"I'm a lawyer. I hate being a lawyer."

I wasn't hearing a question yet, so I waited. He gathered his courage and continued.

"I know I've got more in me than just going to that law office day after day. But I'm scared of really going out and doing something big because the people around me will think I'm showing off or not being grateful for what I have. What do I need to do?"

"That's easy," I assured him.

His eyebrows shot up. Easy?

STEP 5: RELATIONSHIPS

"You've got to change your friend group," I explained. "There is a group of people that is already where you want to go. They will support you, they will embrace you. Your current friend group? They may love you but they aren't giving you the opportunity or the thinking you need in order to grow. You have to change your friend set."

He took it in for a couple of minutes. "Wow," he breathed. "I didn't really think about the people around me in that way. I hadn't considered that I needed to get around new people."

My new friend was clearly a smart guy, being a lawyer and all. But sometimes the most transformational steps we take can be some of the simplest ones. Simply getting the right kind of encouragement from the right people can completely change your landscape.

I'm not saying you have to ditch long-term friendships on the way to your desired destination. What I am saying is that you need the right kind of encouragement to get you there. This lawyer's current friend set encouraged him in the way they knew how. They wanted him to be grateful for what he'd already accomplished. That's not a bad thing. But the right kind of encouragement when it comes to growth and drive is the kind that pushes you in the direction of your potential, that believes you can go farther than you ever have.

You can know that you're in the right rooms when you get the right kind of encouragement, the kind that helps you believe in something bigger instead of the status quo.

The Right Rooms Are Collaborative

Who are you in consistent relationship with who is dreaming big and achieving big? Who are the people who are consistently able to tell you how to do better and, even more importantly, show you how to

FROM DRIFT TO DRIVE

be better? Who in your life has an abundant and generous mindset?

As I continued in my career with Maxwell Leadership, I discovered that the culture of the organization was one where people helped each other, where collaboration was held in high regard, where people were willing to share the resources and insights they had with others. There's not a doubt in my mind that that culture has been intentionally built by John Maxwell. I remember when he started inviting me to join him at the golf course. I would watch him, giving no fanfare and calling no attention to himself, go introduce himself to groundskeepers, food and beverage staff, caddies, and others who were making an afternoon of golf a well-appointed and seamless experience. I saw him quietly and generously tip and chat with people many others might not even notice.

The right rooms are the ones where people are generous with their insights and experience. The right rooms are the ones where you are able to contribute as well. Everyone should be there for the right reasons: learning and growing individually and helping others do the same. If it feels like some kind of beauty competition, or if people who aren't of a certain "status" or accomplishment are treated as "less than," get out of there and find a new team. Character counts, always, no matter how well connected you think a group may be. Generosity, collaboration, cheering for each other, sharing the truth compassionately—those are the marks of a healthy environment.

Kinds of Communities

Now that you know the overall characteristics of the rooms you need to be in, let's get more granular about how to build those relationships and the types of communities available to you.

STEP 5: RELATIONSHIPS

The Cohort Principle

You've likely heard of the term *cohort*. The term originated with the Roman army as a way to describe what today we might think of as a battalion, a specific number of soldiers assigned to each other as a group. They marched together, fought together, pursued the same cause for their country.[52]

Today, a cohort is a group of people who share a defining quality, like age, season of life, or area of expertise. There is power in a cohort. Studies show that learning through a cohort increases your retention of the material you discuss and your odds of completing projects and goals.[53] That was my mistake in that first networking group I was part of. I assumed that because we were all there to work on business ideas, we were a cohort. But in actuality, we weren't. I needed to be part of a community in which we were working together toward similar goals.

Consider whether the groups you're part of today are specific enough for where you are heading. Are the people you're connecting with able to understand what you want to achieve? Do they have enough experience to spot areas where you need help and celebrate areas that are successful for you? For any of the following expressions of relationships, make sure it first passes the cohort test when it comes to the goal you have set for yourself.

Online Communities

Online communities are where I generally recommend people start building relationships specific to their goals. Truly the world is your oyster when it comes to finding others who are doing what you dream of doing, all through the power of the internet. You're

FROM DRIFT TO DRIVE

not constrained by locality or time; you can pop online today, do a quick Google search, and within minutes find a collection of people heading the same direction you are. Communities who are developing careers speaking on specific topics or creating consulting businesses in niche areas of expertise. You'll likely find an incredible set of relationships virtually that can make up the gaps in your local community experience.

An online community can be a fantastic addition to your Relationship step. It gets you outside your local bubble and introduces fresh voices to your endeavors. You'll have the advantage both of the in-person experience and of the ideas and feedback from virtual communities not in your immediate bubble.

In Real Life

IRL, as my kids would text. There's just something so powerful about face-to-face interactions around a shared goal. If you're struggling to find a local group specific to your goals, I'd still encourage you to have some kind of in-person connection. Get off the couch, get out of the house, and talk to real people. Attend events, check out meet-up and affinity groups, get involved in civic organizations.

I have a friend who is part of an in-person mastermind group in his city. It's been a source of fantastic idea-sharing and accountability for several years. Now, that term for this expression of community, *mastermind*, might sound a little daunting to you. My friend would likely laugh about that, particularly if it conjured for you a large think tank. Far from it. This group is made up of four individuals, each of whom has a speaking business, each specializing on a different topic. They meet at one of the mastermind members' homes twice

STEP 5: RELATIONSHIPS

a month. The group and the format aren't complicated or heady, but they are targeted, specific, and goal-centered. While socialization obviously happens, and while these mastermind members care about each other on an interpersonal level, the purpose of the mastermind doesn't waver; they are there to help each other grow and thrive in their speaking careers.

You can do the same. Circle up like-minded people in your town or look for an existing group. While you may at first have to start a bit broader to meet people who share your goals, make the investment to get to know people in your community. You can get more granular as you make those connections. In-person meetings, with clear objectives, can have high innovation and accountability. In a world of social media hype, real connections with real people make a big difference.

Topic-Specific Conferences

I love a good hype session as much as the next person. No question, there's something awe-inspiring and energy-creating about a general conference on personal development and possibility thinking. But I want you to also make sure that you're attending events that are specific to your focused goal. These events might be smaller, with fewer attendees. They might be held in a smaller city, with less razzle-dazzle. The celebrity factor might be lower. But when it comes to moving the needle on your acceleration, topic-specific conferences can be transformative. You'll meet other people who speak the language of your dreams. You'll encounter some who are a few steps ahead of you and others who are a few steps behind. You'll get action-able, definitive direction. And you'll make friends with those who

FROM DRIFT TO DRIVE

can be added to your online community and cohort, an investment in relationships that will carry forward.

Industry-Specific Groups

Connect your vision to an industry, and you'll likely find a community dedicated to that area. Do some research on the finance industry, coaching industry, photography industry, publishing industry, whichever is a fit. The industry in which your dream is housed will often have resources, podcasts, and websites dedicated to it. And within those resources, you just might find people commenting, discussing, and meeting to further their own progress and learning. Around any industry, there are almost always communities that develop in support of that industry. Define your dream's niche, look for services and businesses associated with that niche, and search for the groups that congregate there.

How To Show Up

Just like the filters we talked about for onboarding information back in Step 3, there are relationship filters I want you to install when it comes to achieving your best next thing.

To truly absorb the benefits of relationships that will support you as you reach for your goal, I invite you first to think about the kind of individual you need to be. So often we put an expectation on the relationships around us that they will form us into the best version of ourselves. And make no mistake, I know that our relationships and the quality of those relationships deeply impact who we are. That's why I believe it's so important to be intentional in the relationships we cultivate, and why you'll find so many tools in this

STEP 5: RELATIONSHIPS

chapter on how to choose and evaluate the relationships in your life.

But I'd be doing you no favors if I left it only to that.

How should you be showing up for these relationships? After all, relationships flow both ways. You have responsibilities of your own when it comes to how you connect with others.

Why are you there?

Where I've seen people waste their own time and others' is when they aren't clear about why they are becoming part of particular groups. They're vague about their purpose, and, in return, they get vague results.

For example, I've seen people join a writing community because they want to write a book. They find a group that is kind and supportive. They read each other's work. They cheer each other on. Those are all lovely things. However, if someone's goal is to write a bestselling book, to seek deep and constructive critiques of their work, to land an agent, to learn effective marketing strategies for launching a book, a general writing "support" group isn't going to deliver the desired results.

There's certainly nothing wrong with wanting relationships around you that help you feel good about your writing journey, as long as that's all you're wanting. But if your goal goes further than that, you better believe it's going to take being part of a community that understands that goal and has the right insight and information into how to make that a reality.

What are your goals for being part of this group? Have you clearly communicated that?

FROM DRIFT TO DRIVE

Have you done your research?

What are the values, activities, and culture of the relationship group you are looking at becoming a part of? Just like we talked about earlier, make sure you're in alignment with those from whom you are seeking guidance. The community you surround yourself with in your drive toward your goals should match where you want to go.

Are you willing to be patient?

A mistake I often see people make when it comes to joining a group of like-minded individuals is in expecting immediate results. While I certainly want you to keep an eye on whether being part of a group is bringing you closer to the mindset and practices needed to achieve your goals, it will be a process that takes time.

Are you overcommitting?

When I was new in my journey to becoming a public speaker, there were a couple of groups that I wanted to be a part of because I thought it would help me realize my goal. On paper, these groups seemed to line up right with what I needed, but as I became more involved, something began to emerge that I hadn't expected. Each group had a pretty heavy expectation of volunteering and promotion.

While I do believe you should join a community with a generous heart, you can sometimes find yourself putting in a lot of time dedicated to the furtherance of the group and the initiatives of the group, rather than of your individual vision. Some communities have an expectation that group members will meet multiple times a month, have off-site events multiple times a year, and require fund-raising or administrative duties for the group. Listen, those things

142

STEP 5: RELATIONSHIPS

can all become major distractions from your goal; you must continue to evaluate your progress in the context of the time you're spending. There are other communities out there that will get right to the goal, will honor your time, and will have reasonable expectations about the level of involvement. Keep your commitment to your goal, not one of the vehicles by which you achieve your goal.

Are you curious?

I've felt the pressure. Maybe you have too. You begin to develop new relationships within a community and you want to impress your new friends. You want that social validation that you have accomplished some things in your life, that you are a fun and friendly person. It's normal to share about who you are and what drives you as you develop relationships. But I want to encourage you to keep your curiosity about others and their approaches to the goal as the stronger priority over your personal popularity within the group. Be more interested than interesting.

Are you open?

As humans, we're all susceptible to what is called the *similar-to-me effect*—a tendency to seek out people who remind us of ourselves, whether that's by race, socioeconomic status, education, religion, or culture. But listen: When you open up your life and your capacity to learn from those who are different than you, incredible things can happen. You discover solutions that you and your similar-to-me buddies might never have thought of. You learn about mindsets and approaches you've never considered before.

Now, I can hear you asking how this openness works

FROM DRIFT TO DRIVE

with finding groups and guidance that align with your values and character. But values and character are not the monopolies only of people who look, live, and act like you. Values and character are present across any number of social groups. Be intentional about forming relationships with people from a broad spectrum of life experiences. Your mind, understanding, problem-solving, and general appreciation of humankind will expand exponentially.

Are you being passive or proactive?
A friend of mine was sharing a frustrating experience she had while leading a community group. She had worked very hard to create an inclusive and welcoming environment for new people joining the group; she even had people on her team assigned to help in that process. When new people would show interest in the group, she would immediately assign a team member to show them the ropes, be a personal point of contact, and be someone they could sit with when the group met. It was a great system and worked really well for the most part, helping new group members feel welcome and comfortable.

However, one evening a young woman showed up to the group and resisted sitting with a team member. Multiple people approached her to welcome her. Several people tried to engage her in conversation.

My friend later found her in the lobby of the venue, arms crossed, an angry expression on her face. My friend approached and asked if there was anything wrong. "No one here is friendly," the woman huffed. "I've had a really bad week, and no one is asking

STEP 5: RELATIONSHIPS

about it or asking how they can help." My friend assured her that the group was filled with plenty of caring people and offered to connect her with yet another team member, but the woman was having none of it. She had a passive expectation that the group should somehow read her mind and meet her needs without any prompting. Frankly, she exhibited one of the worst kinds of passivity, the kind that has loads of expectations of others but none for the individual bringing those expectations.

Groups only work so far as you work the group. You have to invest in what's happening. If you expect to receive the full benefit of community, but you're tucked over in a corner, thinking others should be approaching you, thinking it's on everybody else to draw you out, expecting others to come up with a plan and to get your gears in motion, you're going to be disappointed.

Proactivity in community means you communicate, you share, you get out of your comfort zone, you engage. And if there are other members of that community who are intentional in helping those processes, great. But at the end of the day, your group experience is on you, not them. Vet the group you think you want to be a part of, come ready to work, evaluate your progress, give it some time, and track your results. That's on you.

Are you being real?

As my team and I were discussing the mistakes people can make when it comes to being part of a goal-focused community, we reflected on how easy (and how debilitating) it is to show up to a group as someone other than who you really are. It's problematic on a number of levels.

FROM DRIFT TO DRIVE

First, if you truly want to experience growth, feedback, and support from a group, they can't do that for you if they don't know who they're really dealing with. If you're struggling with some confidence issues, how is anyone supposed to help you with that if all you're presenting is that you've got this all buttoned up? If you need help with some details about your goal, but you're showing up acting as if you already know it all, how is someone supposed to know that their expertise is exactly what you need?

There's a difference between *posture* and *imposter*. Look at the cadence, the poetry between those two words. When you show up in the right *posture*, it means you're not coming to a community for them to fix you. You're showing up knowing that you have something to offer the group and they have wisdom and insight to offer you. You don't have to earn your way in, you don't have to strategically impress them. Your posture is such that you know who you are, you have a pretty good idea where you are in relation to your goal, and you know where you want to go.

Imposter, on the other hand? It's when you haven't done the work to feel ready to enter this kind of community. It's when you're still looking for all kinds of outside validation that you even belong in the room. In today's culture we talk a lot about *imposter syndrome*. The term usually describes the emotional experience of when we are filled with self-doubt about what we've achieved, our abilities, and our previous accomplishments.[54]

While I do understand and appreciate the nuances of that definition, I have to tell you: I think there's another kind of imposter syndrome out there. It's the kind that happens when we show up being less than authentic, when we overstate who we are

STEP 5: RELATIONSHIPS

and what we know, when our need to impress outweighs our desire to progress. One more time for the people in the back: **We feel like an imposter when our need to impress outweighs our desire to progress.**

It takes honesty, transparency, and vulnerability to move forward toward something we haven't done before. Not only do you not have to show up to a new community with all the answers—you shouldn't. If you're the person in the room with the most experience and most insight, you're in the wrong room. If you feel like you have to *act* like the person in the room with the most experience and insight, you're not ready for the room. Posture versus imposter, it's up to you.

* * *

While human interaction is layered, complex, and fascinating, pursuing goal-intentional relationships can be distilled into three steps: Select, Connect, Engage.

- **Select,** with clarity and intentionality, the kinds of rooms and the kinds of people who can take you toward your goals.

- **Connect**, with generosity, kindness, and honesty, with the communities you select.

- **Engage**, with consistency, open-mindedness, and proactivity, in the accountability and feedback in the relationships you establish.

The power of the Tour de France, the famous bike race that happens over three weeks mainly through France each summer, happens because of a particular phenomenon.

FROM DRIFT TO DRIVE

The cyclists speed down the road in a cluster, wheels almost touching, the road flying beneath their wheels. When they enter this kind of cluster formation, it's known as the peloton. There's an efficiency, a power that happens when the peloton forms. Your speed increases as a group. You are 40 percent more efficient as you ride. You're shielded from oppressive winds and drag is significantly reduced, all by riding within a group headed to the same finish line.[55]

The fifth step of Relationships, of this particular kind of relationship, at this stage and season of your journey, will align you, shoulder to shoulder, with others headed the same direction. The things that would slow you down were you to continue to go solo will be mitigated. The encouragement and pace of the community will help you drive harder. The companionship on the road will encourage you. Don't skip this powerful part of the framework. When you advance toward your dream in a caravan, the miles are all the sweeter and your effort is all the more enhanced.

STEP 6: ACTION
One Mile at a Time

....

I want you to enjoy the excitement you've been developing in the previous parts of the framework. I want you to experience the energy of taking action on what you've been dreaming and learning and connecting with. And I want you to take on the step of Action with a simple strategy and with intention, overcoming what I call two-speed transmission thinking.

When I work with people to help them overcome complacency and head toward a new dream, this step always prompts the question, *What action should I take first?* I understand. You've taken on a lot of new information. You've closely examined the work and impact of others on a similar journey. You're standing at the edge, but

FROM DRIFT TO DRIVE

taking that first action step?

It can feel daunting, overwhelming, confusing. Or all three.

Here's what I tell people:

Take the next easiest step.

By the end of this chapter, you'll have the tools you need to do just that.

Overcoming Two-Speed Thinking

We've already established that I love cars. Nice cars. Fancy cars. Exotic cars. I love to go car shopping. I love to check out the latest designs and features. I love to go to a great car show and check out plush interiors and admire the latest paint options and finishes. But as I also mentioned earlier, I'm not *that* kind of car guy, the guy who knows all the ins and out of engines and gears and pumps and belts. I leave that stuff in the hands of the professionals.

The experts will tell you that you and I likely drive cars that have multispeed transmissions. Your transmission is what sends the power from the engine into the wheels, moving your car forward. With a multispeed transmission, cars are able to access different speeds from the power of the engine as needed as we head down the road and into different driving situations. (You likely experience this when climbing or descending a hilly road.)

But some smaller cars, tractors, and heavy driving equipment often have what's known as a two-speed transmission. It's a cheaper system that takes up less space in the vehicle. It's pretty straightforward, with one gear for going slow and another for going faster. A two-speed transmission means you only have one of two power settings available, while a multispeed transmission gives you a range

STEP 6: ACTION

of power options.

What does all this have to do with overcoming drift in your life, keeping you in the lane of your dreams?

I'm glad you asked.

In this next complacency-busting step, you're going to discover how to get the power of your engine, that information and guidance and relationship momentum you've developed with the previous steps, to the wheels. And you'll learn how to overcome the two-speed transmission settings that hinder a lot of people from ever getting to their destination.

Setting #1: Overdrive

I've done it. I bet you have too.

I get inspired to go for a new level of fitness. I catch up on the latest research on exercise routines and nutrition. I have a coach show me a few things. I make a pact with my buddy to meet at the gym.

That's when it all goes sideways.

Because that's when I decide that, in the name of wanting to see big results, I should lift all the things and run on all the things and row on all the things and squat all the things. In my effort to overcome the drift in my personal fitness training, I jam the pedal from zero to seventy-five, all on a Monday morning.

When I pull a stunt like that, by Tuesday morning, I can barely hobble out of bed.

Sound familiar?

There's just something in our human nature that, once we start to get fired up about a new destination, we confuse focus with frenzy and start throwing everything we've got into the fray.

FROM DRIFT TO DRIVE

I want you to get really honest with yourself about how you approach Action. I have friends who say about themselves, "I have two settings: full on or full stop!" I appreciate their honesty. And I know that that kind of two-speed transmission thinking will only get them so far before their engine burns out.

Taking action isn't about trying to do everything all at once.

Let me give you an example of what that has looked like in my life.

When I decided to really go for it with my speaking and coaching career with Maxwell Leadership, I needed to throw everything I had at it. I knew that at that time, I needed my coaching business to generate $4,000 a month. It was tempting to frantically run day and night to accomplish that. There was a mortgage to pay and a bunch of babies to be fed, and it could have been easy to let my anxiety run the show with two-speed transmission thinking. Instead, I used a different gear.

When it comes to taking the next easiest step in the Action phase, there's a principle I want you to memorize:

To multiply your actions, you must first divide.

When I sat with the reality that I needed to earn $4,000 in income to make my dream financially viable, I could have gotten stuck on taking the first step because $4,000 extra a month seemed insurmountable. Too big. Too broad a step to attempt. But I looked at it from a different angle, from a point of dividing.

Okay, $4,000 was ten clients, each of whom would pay $400 a month for my coaching services.

Now let's divide again.

What step do I need to take today to get one client of those

STEP 6: ACTION

ten? One person who needs the services I'm offering and is ready to invest in their future?

Now I was getting somewhere.

The next easiest step was to make the calls needed to find that one client at $400. Once I found that one client, I then took the action again to find the next client. Then I repeated those same steps to find the third client, and so on.

Look at how each major goal could be divided into the action I needed to take next:

Goal: Be a professional speaker and coach

Divided by: The financial reality that is needed for ultimately accomplishing my goal

Equals: $4,000 a month in coaching clients to supplement speaking income

Now keep going...

Goal: $4,000 a month in coaching income

Divided by: Specific number of new clients

Equals: Book one new client at $400 per month, then do it again nine more times

I'm not claiming to be some kind of math whiz but it's an exercise you can quickly do to help you determine that easiest next step. Notice that I didn't spin my wheels worrying about how to get to a hundred clients or what kind of support staff I would need if I hit that number or wondering if first I should rent office space that would reflect having a big coaching business. I simply needed to put the car into first gear, get a little acceleration, then move to the next

FROM DRIFT TO DRIVE

gear, and then the next. That's the acceleration you're looking for, friend. It's there, in a multispeed approach, not in the wheels-on-fire frenzy.

Setting #2: Too Slow

A friend of mine told the story of being on a trip with her family when she was a kid. They visited an amusement park that had a cave as one of the experiences. This cave was man-made, but there were "warning" signs about a bottomless pit and to be careful not to get lost because parts of the cave were "unknown and unexplored." My friend, being the age she was, bought it hook, line, and sinker. While the rest of her family walked through the cave, my friend stopped, frozen at the entrance. Her family didn't realize she wasn't with them until they popped out the other side. Their panic in trying to find her turned to frustration and irritation when they realized that she was still at the entrance, unwilling to move, a line forming behind her.

That's the image that comes to mind for me when I see someone work beautifully through all the other phases of the framework and then get stuck at the Action step.

Are there things that are still unknown up ahead? Sure. Are there some chills and thrills as you take the next step and then the next? Likely. But it's taking that first step that carries you to the next and then the next.

Take the next easiest step.

Okay, that might sound easier said than done. But think about it. The temptation to overanalyze the "right" next step into action can keep you frozen. Sometimes that looks like doubling back to do some more research or to get one more opinion. But, friend, at some

STEP 6: ACTION

point, if you're ever going to progress, you've got to make a move.

To get to where I was going in building my coaching and speaking business, I needed to take that first step into the cave, so to speak. I needed that one client. Then another one. And then another.

The Road of Steady Progress

When I set my sights on achieving a new level I'd never reached before, I worked my way through the Gathering and Filtering steps, and I was diligent in forming guidance and cohort relationships. But I knew I had the potential to get stuck when it came to taking action.

My solution? First I signed up for a course to help build my speaking and coaching business. Now, I'll admit ahead of time that this next part probably isn't for the faint of heart. What I can also tell you is that it works, whether your problem is a tendency to go too fast, or to be hesitant to move forward.

Here's what I did.

I'd watch a training video. And the minute someone on the video said, "Go do this," I'd stop the video, right there, and go take that action. Sometimes that action would take me a few minutes and sometimes it would take several days. Regardless, I would not allow myself to move ahead in the video until I had completed the action given up to that point.

I know that can sound scary to some people. They want to know every turn in the road, every railroad crossing, before they ever head out on the journey. I get it, but I also want you to consider if that could be holding you back. For me, when I tried to take in the entirety of a video training, I tended to want to skip the earliest steps and jump ahead to what I saw as the "meat" of the training.

FROM DRIFT TO DRIVE

The problem was, those early steps, the ones that didn't feel all that monumental or epic to me, were actually laying the groundwork for what would come next. When I skipped ahead, inserted my own editing into the process or allowed myself to get distracted, I made the action decision process more complicated than it needed to be.

Hence my simple recipe: hearing an action, stopping the video, taking the action, and only then returning to the video.

I've noticed that when people freeze or frenzy when it comes to taking action, it's often because of a myth that pops up or because they're freewheeling a recipe. What does that mean? Consider the following if you find you don't know what action to take or you don't know what to do next.

Ditching the Myth of THE Way

Santa Claus. The Easter Bunny. The Tooth Fairy.

When it comes to taking action, you might have to kick these cats to the door.

Did Chris just suggest that I kick Santa?

No, not really. But these mythical figures serve as a metaphor for where you might find yourself getting stuck on taking the next easiest step. Each of these characters represents THE way you get your stocking filled and presents under the tree, get your Easter basket packed to the brim with chocolate, and exchange your baby teeth for some cold hard cash. When we were kids, these characters represented the one way to get us to those results.

Today, you've likely moved on from these holiday fables, but you might be approaching taking action toward your dreams the same way. That's because you may have bought into the myth that

156

STEP 6: ACTION

there is one, and only one, right way to approach your dream. You send yourself on a scavenger hunt, careening down all kinds of rabbit trails, to discover this legendary path. *Sure, Chris, I'll take action, just as soon as I find the one magical path that will ensure my success, will create the least amount of challenge, and will guarantee extraordinary profits in the first year.*

Here's some truth that will set you free.

When it comes to achieving your potential, there is not just *a* way. There are *multiple* ways. You just need to pick one. And stick with it. Like I did with the course I chose.

Freewheeling in the Action Kitchen

Who doesn't love a great cook? I have some people in my life who could show up at your house on a random weekend, take a look in your pantry and fridge, and with no recipe cards, no cookbook, nothing, whip up an amazing meal to enjoy. They say things like, "I'll just put in a pinch of this and a dab of that and a handful of shredded cheese," and somehow, something incredible ends up on your plate. It's admirable and part magic and makes you want to cook the same way.

Listen, what you do in your kitchen on a random weekend is up to you, but I'm telling you loud and clear here, do *not* take the same approach when it comes to the step of Action.

I've worked with several individuals who muddy their path because they simply won't commit to a way. We'll start with a good heading. They'll choose a program or training to follow. And then, the next time we meet, they'll tell me about this other action they've added to the mix from this other expert or program. They want to

FROM DRIFT TO DRIVE

sprinkle in this ingredient or ratchet up the oven temp a few more degrees, so to speak.

Guess what?

Not only are they making the whole thing more complicated, and possibly take more time, they're also throwing all these actions in so on the fly that they'll likely never replicate the results. I'm sure you see it at play in your day-to-day life. A friend says they want to lose weight. They start out on a low-fat diet but four days in decide that maybe they should add this soup they heard about on TikTok that might heal their liver. And then a few days after that, they decide they'll go high protein. And a month later, they've ditched the whole thing in favor of some new smoothie. They say they have a desired outcome in mind, but they're trying to make it all up as they go, sabotaging their efforts by piling in more and more approaches.

The Action step is not about improv. It's about intentionally choosing a way of action, doing that action, and observing. (We'll talk more about this last aspect shortly.)

As we talked about earlier, I'm a big proponent of Learn a Little, Do a Little. You can see that reflected in my method of pausing the video and taking the next step. The reason I believe Learn a Little, Do a Little is so powerful is because it can take what could seem overwhelming and make it actionable. It's division in real time, and it helps you to stay on task a step at a time. And guess what? A series of Learn a Littles compound into you having learned a lot.

Another reason I want you to think of action as a series of small steps is because, when you start getting results, I want you to know how you got them. Imagine if someone came up with a way to turn, say, used coffee grounds into literal gold. That would be

STEP 6: ACTION

pretty amazing, right? But if they were just throwing random things into their chemistry beaker, if they changed things up all the time, they'd never be able to trace their way back to how they got that gold outcome. You and I, we want to understand, study, and be able to repeat the great results we get when we take an action. And when we don't get an expected result, we want to be able to retrace our steps to understand why.

Some action steps along the way are going to stretch you more than others. There will be some places where you'll have to take a leap of faith. But make no mistake: The first easiest step is still massive action. It still puts gears in the engine. It matters. Small steps are big moments in the development of your momentum.

The Fraternal Twins of Inaction

They don't look much alike, but they're twins, alright. Procrastination and perfectionism, two sides of the same coin.

When someone comes to me and tells me they're stuck at the Action step, that they just don't know what to do next, I encourage them to go back to Filtering and then to Guidance. Usually, they haven't chosen a reasonable set of steps to follow, and I often find that filtering the information they've gathered for a specific template of action, and then seeking the action steps of someone for whom they've identified as a guide in their journey, will do the trick. This is also where the index card method I showed you in Step 3 comes into play, breaking down the day's actions into five categories:

1. What do I need to read today?

2. What do I need to listen to today?

FROM DRIFT TO DRIVE

3. Who do I need to call today?

4. What do I need to do today?

5. What am I looking for today?

But sometimes a person claims to have gone back through those steps and the index card method and is still stuck. While I certainly don't claim to be a therapist, I've seen this enough to know that they are very likely stuck because of procrastination, perfectionism, or both.

Procrastination shows up in lots of forms. It can look like putting off an important phone call because first you "really" need to tidy your desk. It can look like falling down a rabbit hole of scrolling social media or websites and calling it *research*. It can look like everything from pulling the covers over your head instead of taking on the day to getting a million tiny things done on your to-do list, none of which move you closer to your goal.

Perfectionism, on the other hand, is paralyzing. Like we talked about earlier in this chapter, perfectionism tries to convince you that there's THE way to do something, and if you can't discover it or do it perfectly, then you're stuck. Perfectionism is terrified to paint the first stroke on the canvas, make the first pitch with the new deck, set the price point where it needs to be because *what if I do it wrong?*

If you don't ever encounter these twin forces, good for you. But for many of us, we can feel the tug when we get ready to take a new step. That's when procrastination or perfectionism typically love to show up. And for some people, procrastination and perfectionism show up together on loop. Psychologists say that, while procrastination can stand on its own, perfectionism can often lead to

STEP 6: ACTION

procrastination, and then you're double-stuck, another reflection of the limitations of two-speed transmission thinking.[56]

I sometimes find that when someone is resisting taking action, either from a position of procrastination or perfectionism, they're held captive by all the questions they have: *Am I doing the right thing? Am I doing it the right way? What will the outcome be?*

Guess what holds the answers to those questions?

Action.

When you take action, it always answers questions. Sometimes you'll like the answers. Sometimes you won't. Regardless, one action begets another. You take an action and it gives you the information you need for the next action.

If you're looking for certainty before you take action, either to quell perfectionism or to stave off procrastination, I want to encourage you to let that go. Certainty is a signpost on the way to complacency; risk is the mileage sign on the way to the top. Put another way, you can be certain you'll be taking some risks to go for your dreams.

When someone self-diagnoses to me, stating, "Well, I'm stuck because I'm just such a perfectionist," or "I've always been such a procrastinator, so I'm back in the same fight with this new goal," I believe them. But I also think it's important to know that there can be some things beneath the surface that are causing that perfectionism or procrastination.

What I often find rippling under those explanations for not taking action is *fear*. Fear of being disappointed if things don't turn out the way you hope. Fear of looking dumb for trying. Fear of spending time or resources on something when there aren't guarantees. Fear of

FROM DRIFT TO DRIVE

the unknown. And there's also the fear of the *known*, when you know you have more potential inside you, but you fear how others might perceive you or judge you for making another run at the summit.

Now, let's flip all those heavy things for better thoughts. Let's shift into multispeed thinking:

- You don't have to take perfect action: Take *an* action.

- You don't have to wait to take a step until you have all the answers: Take action.

- You can feel the fear and still move forward: Take action.

Action carries its own power. When you take action, you are telling your negative thoughts, *I can do this. I can try. I can get up again.* The more action you take, the more your mind experiences the positive rewiring that better inoculates it against perfectionism, fear, and procrastination. Action is the antidote to a hesitant mindset. Action is the medicine for complacency. Celebrate each action that you take. It's a great brain hack; when you celebrate, when you are encouraging to yourself for each action you take, you're raising your dopamine. You're literally creating connections in your brain that will make it easier to take the next action, and then the next.

Peeking Too Soon

No, that's not a misspelling. Sure, we talk about someone *peak*ing too soon, for example, when an athlete gives their peak performance at the practice before the big game or when someone has an early success and then doesn't do much after. No, what I'm talking about is truly *peeking* too soon at the results you're getting from your actions.

A friend of mine made a significant investment in a coaching

STEP 6: ACTION

program to help him raise a significant amount of money for a nonprofit he's passionate about. A month and a half into the program, he called me, worried and frustrated.

"I think I may need to do something else," he shared. "It's just not working."

"Slow down," I advised. "Tell me what's going on."

"Well, I've been at it for forty-five days and I've only raised $5,000! That's so far away from my goal that I've got to reconsider what I'm doing here! And I invested a hefty amount of money into this training program. I've got to be able to justify that expense, and raising a measly 5,000 bucks just isn't going to cut it!"

My friend was making a classic error: peeking too soon and applying what he found there disproportionately. He was underestimating the positive impact of his small wins and overemphasizing how far he had to go to meet his ultimate goal.

As we continued to talk, I shared this with him. "Listen, all you really need to know right now is that you've got a result. The action you have taken has led to an outcome. That's great! If you were to continue practicing the same action, you will have raised a solid five figures by the end of the year."

"But that's not even close to what I need to raise!" he spluttered.

"Whoa, whoa, hold on." I reminded him, "In taking consistent action, in giving it time, you will likely encounter more and more donors. Those donors have relationships they'll likely connect you with. You'll get better and better at the action you're taking, and that will also open doors. Right now, you're early in. You're trying to peek into the next twelve months too soon. You're taking action, you're getting a result. For right now, that's all you need to know."

FROM DRIFT TO DRIVE

Does there come a time when you need to evaluate the results you're getting? Absolutely, and we'll be uncovering that in the next step of the framework. But I want to warn you at the Action phase that, for a little while, you simply won't have enough data yet to truly paint a full picture.

Spending my childhood in Oklahoma City and in St. Louis, my hometowns were surrounded by wide tracts of farmland. There's a wisdom in the cycle of those crops. Every good farmer knows that there is a gestation period specific to the crop you want to grow. For example, let's say I wanted to grow corn. Now, I might think that I have a great new strategy for getting the outcome I desire, a harvest of mature corn. But I decide that I'm going to speed things up and throw in some different techniques. I plant those corn kernels and I water them for three days straight. I dump pounds and pounds of fertilizer on my seeds. I throw in some things I've heard have worked on soybean crops and wheat crops. I expect to see fast and big results, and I want to hurry things up.

The result? The corn still won't be ready until high July.

Why? Crops, babies, ideas, dreams, achievements, they all come with a gestation period, that investment of time required to bring something to its harvest. Jenee and I felt the power of the gestation period keenly when we were expecting our triplets. Our doctors continued to remind us that the longer Jenee could carry the babies, the better, that as close as we could get them to the needed gestation period, the better for their health and the maturity of their lungs. The repeated actions on Jenee's part of good nutrition, hydration, and rest were the actions needed to help deliver our triplets. And a few years later our singleton. And then our twins.

STEP 6: ACTION

Gestation.

Am I suggesting that you not look for ways to be more efficient? Not at all. Am I saying that you can't figure out a faster way from looking at the journey of someone who has gone before you? Nope. But don't get sidelined or sidetracked from your main mission.

Too often, we determine our discipline toward a goal by the level of sustained enthusiasm or excitement we have for it. While I certainly hope you find fulfillment in your efforts and are excited when you reach your goal, it's my greater hope that in the process, you don't allow your emotions to become the barometer. When you peek too early into what your actions are creating, you're putting yourself at risk to allow what you think you see there to become the driver. It looks like you're getting traction after just a couple of action steps? You might do what I've done at the gym, pouring too much gasoline and burning out. You don't see any progress after a couple of action steps? You might find it harder to pick up that phone and make your calls the next day.

Let's go back to that example of me growing corn (although, I have to admit, the idea of me being a corn farmer would give my nearest and dearest a good laugh). If I planted those corn kernels, but then every day I went out and dug them back up to see how things were going, instead of focusing on keeping the field weeded and the deer and rabbits off the premises, I'd undo what I was trying to do.

Again, there is a time to look at results. But don't confuse an early obsession with looking for results with taking action.

A few years ago, I was contacted by a salesperson in the luxury pen business. He showed me a beautiful collection of the world's finest pens, the kind that have a price tag attached that can make your eyes

FROM DRIFT TO DRIVE

water. He went through his whole presentation and at the end of his pitch, I bought an ink cartridge from him. A $15 ink cartridge.

Now, if that sales guy had peeked too early, had looked at that $15 sale and thought it was the whole story, that likely would have been the end of line. Instead, he kept taking action steps. A thoughtful email here. A phone call there. A handwritten card on occasion. And now, over the years, when I've wanted to purchase a high-end gift for someone, guess who I've called? My pen guy, the person who stayed in the lane, took the actions, allowed the relationship to gestate, and was consistent over time, which led to me spending more and more dollars with him.

* * *

Because I am someone who truly believes in the power of mindset, and because I truly believe you have it in you to leave complacency behind and move powerfully into your next season, I have to admit I'm a little hesitant to bring up this statistic. But I think it's a really important one that brings home the importance of taking things a step at a time, giving it time, and doing the action time and again. Recent research has shown that only 8 percent of people reach their goals.[57] I know. That's a tough piece of data to read for people like you and me, people who drive harder and reach farther. But let's remember, it's not a prophecy. There are solid reasons why 92 percent of people don't accomplish what they set out to do.

And when you flip it around, there are solid reasons why that 8 percent do reach where they're aiming.

Setting a specific goal. Check.

STEP 6: ACTION

Gathering and absorbing pertinent information. Check.

Having guidance. Check.

Developing a great support system. Check.

Taking specific, targeted action and being consistent. Check.

These are all things that the 8 percent do differently. And when you follow the framework you've studied in this book, you're in that 8 percent. You'll make your drive to your dreams and be able to accommodate for bumps in the road, unexpected curves, and uneven conditions. You'll be able to take all the heart and excitement for your goal and turn it into the action, the power, that turns your wheels in the direction of your destiny.

The Action step is mission critical to you getting to your destination. One step at a time takes you to your dreams.

I want to close out this chapter with a few fantastic quotes that I'd encourage you to put on your screen saver, on a Post-it note on your mirror, or a piece of paper on your fridge.

"An ounce of action is worth a ton of theory."
RALPH WALDO EMERSON

"Small deeds done are better than great deeds planned."
PETER MARSHALL

"Be consistent every day that ends with 'day.'"
CHRIS ROBINSON

The synergy of information and action unleashes potential and drives achievement. In taking action on information, outcomes and solutions are realized. It's as simple and as big as that.

STEP 7: EVALUATING
Four Questions That Keep You on Target

. . . .

I'm a father of six kids.

Six.

Kids.

That's a lot of kids.

My wife, Jenee, and I love being parents and are so grateful for our children. Our path to building a family was a tough one in the beginning, and we don't take a minute of our family life for granted.

Now, as a father of six, I can tell you, I get to repeat myself. A lot.

"Take your shoes to your room."

FROM DRIFT TO DRIVE

"You, stop fighting with your brother! And, you, stop fighting with your sister!"

"Say please."

"Did you make your bed?"

"I said," (*again*), "stop fighting."

"You need to finish your science project by *what* time tomorrow morning?!? And you need posterboard and paint to do it?"

It seems like the business world has recently discovered a phrase that Jenee and I have already known to be true through our years of parenting a big crew.

You can't expect what you won't inspect.

That kid who tells you they'll clean their room before they play a video game? They might really intend to do it, but you can't just assume it's going to happen. Believe me, when you announce that you're going to inspect their room, you'll likely hear a lot of drawers opening and closing and closet doors slamming as you make your way down the hall.

Why?

Because there's power in the inspection. There's power in taking a good hard look at what has taken place in the aftermath of committing to an action.

You've arrived at the Evaluation step. This is an opportunity to inspect what you expect from yourself, from the efforts you've put forth in your drive to your goals. You created GPS directions for yourself when you headed out on this journey. This is the time when you step out of the vehicle for a moment and check to see how things are going.

STEP 7: EVALUATING

Understand, Inspect, Modify

The Evaluation step is a series of four questions designed to help you understand, inspect, and modify the actions you've taken. The Action and Evaluation steps run on loop together: You take an action, you get a result, you evaluate that result, you modify an action that needs modifying, and you repeat an action that has yielded a fruitful result.

This isn't about running around in a circle; this is the circular motion of a well-guided wheel keeping you not only in the lane but in motion toward your goal.

There are a couple of things to note before you run your first results through evaluation from the action you took based on the last chapter.

First, laying out a course of action is not the same thing as taking that action. It is only in taking the action that you will get a result. You've got to have a result in order to move on to evaluating that result. Have you worked your way through your index card? Have you placed the phone call, made the offering, posted the content? You don't evaluate what you've *talked* about doing, you evaluate *what you've actually done.*

Secondly, do you remember in the previous chapter when we talked about choosing *a* way, not getting caught up in the mythology of trying to find *THE* way? Results follow the same math. A result is *a* result, not *the* result. All results can go through the Evaluation step and be modified. Results can be improved through evaluation.

I'm going to ask you to do two things at once that might at first seem contradictory. I'm going to ask you, simultaneously, to *unemotionally* observe the results you've received while also maintaining your *passion* for the ultimate goal you have for yourself. There's an

FROM DRIFT TO DRIVE

alchemy that really is important—being able to stare down a result without letting it discourage you while keeping your energy and excitement high for where you're headed.

Remember, you've gotten *a* result, and it's a result you can either replicate exactly or shape differently in the next round of actions you take.

Now let's dive into the four questions of Evaluation:

1. What did I do?

2. What did I learn?

3. What did I like?

4. What would I change or do differently?

Let's break those down individually.

1. *What Did I Do?*

When my family was making the move from Saint Louis to Palm Beach, Florida, the movers helping us were worth every penny. Why? Because as I've told you, I've got books everywhere, a stack always going. As more and more boxes were filled with books, and as those heavy boxes were then hustled down the stairs and out the door, one of the movers remarked to me, "You've got so many books! So many!"

If he and I had had the opportunity to sit down over coffee, what I would have shared with him is this:

Success leaves clues.

All those books? That collection is a clue for what I've been able to accomplish.

You've already been gathering many clues in working through

STEP 7: EVALUATING

the previous steps, but those clues have come from external sources, like books, mentors, and cohorts. Now, I want you to look to your own approaches and results for those clues.

You've taken an action.

You now have a result.

What did you do to get that result?

As you ask yourself that, I'd like you to leave the idea of if the result is a good or bad one on the back burner for now. At this point, I simply want you to make sure you know the recipe for the current result you've experienced. It might be that you watched a coaching video, you took the first step outlined in that video, and you got a result. Or maybe, as a result of ideas from your time in the Guidance and Relationship elements of the framework, you made five outbound sales calls each day for a week using a template from a mentor or peer, and you now have a result to evaluate. However you got to a result, take some time to write down everything you did to get that result. That becomes the baseline as you move forward for evaluating what to keep in your repertoire and what to let go of.

2. What Did I Learn?

This is as straightforward as it sounds, and yet, it's often something people forget to think about. Anytime you undertake an action, and when that action gives you a result, there's something to learn there. It might be just one or two things, or it might be many. Regardless, you want to pay attention to that learning curve.

Begin by writing down the things you've learned that pop out first to you. Perhaps you learned that making those five phone calls didn't take as long as you thought. Maybe you learned that finding coaching clients was harder than you expected or simpler than you anticipated. What are the things that you discovered in the process of taking this particular action?

3. What Did I Like?

There are going to be things you need to do to achieve your dream that aren't always fun and that will push you out of your comfort zone. One of the biggest misconceptions I see today in working with clients is that they have been sold a falsehood that everything about their goals should be fun and should feel easy.

Wrong.

But I also don't buy into the idea that you're going to have to suffer, suffer, suffer to get to where you want to go. There should be fun along the way. You should like a lot of what you get to do. What's the point in building toward something you don't even enjoy?

That's why I want you to jot down what you liked in the action that you have taken as you evaluate your results. You may find that something you didn't think you would like doing you actually ended up enjoying. You might also discover that something you thought you would like turned out not to be as exciting or as interesting as you thought. In the Evaluation step, when you take the time to really think about what you liked in the action you took, it will help you home in further on those things you want to spend the bulk of your time doing and those things you might want to delegate. It helps give you a more accurate picture of who you are in general and who you are in relation to your goals.

For example, I know people in the speaking world who thought they would really like the public recognition and fame they thought

STEP 7: EVALUATING

they would receive. Some of them ultimately discovered that what they *really* liked was the development of the material, practicing that material, and tweaking it after each presentation. What they thought would drive them farther in their goal actually ended up not being the thing that they liked the most. This didn't mean they needed to stop driving in their dream for public speaking. It simply meant that they now knew that preparation and research was what they liked best and that that aspect of taking action was an important part of their enjoyment. When you're clear on what you like in the process of getting results, it helps you gain even greater understanding as you move forward about what actions feel best to you.

4. What Would I Change or Do Differently?

I love pickleball. So much. I started playing in 2020 and never looked back. And if running around on a court chasing a little ball with a paddle under the hot Florida sun is wrong, then I don't wanna be right.

Pickleball has been the fastest-growing sport in the United States over the last three years and the number of people playing just keeps on growing.[58] For myself, I started out playing just to hang out with friends and to see what everyone around me seemed to be so fired up about. *Okay, simmer down. It's just a sort of "little tennis."*

But then the pickleball virus took hold of me and now I just can't get enough court time. I'm coaching and playing and in tournaments and I'm for sure a picklehead at this point.

One of the things I like best about pickleball?

There's always something to adjust and improve, things as simple as tweaking your paddle a couple of degrees or running laps around the track to give you better endurance on the court.

FROM DRIFT TO DRIVE

During each pickleball match I play, my brain is on alert for what I can change in the next volley, in what I can do differently the next time I'm up to serve. It's part of the fun of the game, celebrating when I score the point, learning when my shot goes over the line.

Think of the actions you're taking toward your vision as a pickleball match (you are playing pickleball these days, right?). You hit the ball (an action) and you see where it goes (evaluation). You observe how it's received on the other side of the net (an apt metaphor when your actions are moving you toward your customer or audience) and then you adjust your next swing, based on what you learn from their response.

It's a real-time, act-evaluate-adjust moment right there.

Every now and then, someone will interpret this question of *What would I change or do differently?* as a call to be hypercritical of the action they took. Don't do that to yourself. At the same time, even if you are completely happy with the action and result you experienced, push yourself a bit to define some micro adjustments you can make the next time you act. Too often, we either avoid making any upgrades in our actions because we're afraid we'll mess up, or we want to scrap everything and start over completely, ignoring that we've usually got some grains of goodness mixed in.

* * *

Keep the lines distinct: Know what you did to get the result, define what you learned in the process, clarify what you liked in what you did, and look for what you want to change or do differently the next go-around.

STEP 7: EVALUATING

These four questions that you ask yourself about your observations following the actions you take toward your goals are how you begin to build a process and refine that process. The answers help you create replicable patterns moving forward. Walking through the four questions of the Evaluation step develops your expertise in what you are creating.

Evaluation Errors

I often think of Evaluation as one of the most powerful phases of the Seven Step Framework because it's where all the other steps you've taken come together and you catch your first glimpse of the broader landscape. Scanning the results of who you've talked to, what you've read, and what you've done to reach these results, you start to see the bigger picture of all that effort.

But I also know that this time of evaluation is a place where people can get stuck afresh, mired in a bog of issues. The purpose of evaluation is to empower you for what comes next, not disempower you with doubt. As you spend some time looking at the results you've gained so far, here's how to avoid the top issues I see crop up in the Evaluation step.

Don't focus only on the end goal.

But, Chris, you're the guy who told me to pick a point on the horizon and go for it! Yes, and I stand by that. But if you only evaluate what your journey has been like to this point based on whether or not you've arrived, you will have missed all the insight and equipping along the way.

What I've found is that when someone misses or ignores the

FROM DRIFT TO DRIVE

information they get through the evaluation process, or when they are only willing to evaluate the results they've created through a lens of "Am I there yet?" they hamstring themselves moving forward.

Sometimes this is a symptom of a larger issue. Part of the purpose of going through the Seven Step Framework is to break down each action you're going to take toward your big goal. This means that, just like the way I told you I watched that teaching video series, you determine a step, "pause" on mixing in any other actions, take the step you've determined, get a result, and then evaluate that result. Step by step by step. However, sometimes people take a bunch of smaller actions and don't take the time to evaluate them, instead waiting until they think they're at the end goal to look back and evaluate. Don't do this. You'll rob yourself of valuable information along the way, and you're missing a crucial central feature of this book, which is taking measured, informed steps of action to create sustainable, directed, intentional momentum, one of the best complacency busters I know.

Look, I want you moving into new territory and new horizons, not sitting in a parking lot under a *Done* billboard. So many exciting things are happening as a result of the actions you've taken; don't miss them. Evaluate each and every action, as they each give you a result.

Don't ignore the small wins.

If you've set any kind of health and fitness goal, you know that experts will tell you over and over that you're not going to lose all the weight in a week.

The same goes for your goals for your next dream.

Oh, sure, you probably legitimately do have someone in your world who has managed to achieve microwave-quick success that

STEP 7: EVALUATING

exceeds all the usual growth curves and growing pains. But for most of us, success is built brick by brick, one action at a time, evaluated and adjusted to then lay the next brick.

Every brick you lay? That's a celebration.

But too often you and I put off seeing the small wins. We only think it really "counts" when we hit a certain level in sales or in bookings.

Lean in now, because this is important.

Those small wins? Getting up each day, being consistent in making the calls you need to make, checking off items on your index card? Those are the embers that fuel you to keep moving forward. When you celebrate the small wins, when you take the time to notice the small results and to see their value, you're stoking the fires of momentum that will keep you progressing toward your goal.

Don't compare yourself to others around you.

I know, I know. And you do too. We say it all the time, that we can't compare ourselves to others, that what we see in their lives is the highlight reel, that when we traffic in comparison we're letting it steal joy from us.

I know that's all true.

And I also know it's hard not to do.

It makes me think about when I'm minding my own business, driving through town, staying in my lane. And then it happens. Somebody comes riding up on my bumper. They gun their engine. They swing around me as if I'm going twenty miles under the speed limit. They keep pace with me in the adjacent lane, revving their engine a couple more times. Then they shoot through the next yellow light as I'm starting to brake, just to prove they can.

FROM DRIFT TO DRIVE

Something about that makes you want to gun your own engine, play chicken at the next traffic light, prove what kind of horsepower you've got under the hood. Right?

But…why?

Who cares if that random driver can drive faster and spends more on his car budget? After all, isn't the goal to get where I'm going, not to race against him?

Comparison makes us doubt the vehicle of our vision, gets us focused on the unimportant, makes us think there's some kind of competition brewing. It ultimately has us gunning toward a destination we never intended, all at the risk of having some parking lot altercation with a stranger. Metaphorically, of course.

How someone else is doing is no indication of how you're doing. While I typically think we tend to compare "up"—allowing ourselves to feel less than because of what someone else is accomplishing—there's also the lure of comparing "down"—congratulating ourselves on what we've done because it's better than so-and-so.

Either way: Who cares?

If you find comparison showing up in the Evaluation step, know this: It's a driving distraction. It gets your eyes off your lane, and it can drive you into a ditch where you're spinning your wheels. You're evaluating *your* results based on the road *you've* laid out for *yourself.* It doesn't matter how fast or slow, big or small someone else is doing things. What matters are your actions and how they're getting you to your destination. Don't fall for the primal call of an engine revving next to yours. Stay in your lane, stay true to yourself.

STEP 7: EVALUATING

Don't set unrealistic timelines.

You and I both know that a lot of parameters surrounding goal setting include deadlines. And while having some kind of time frame identified in a goal-setting process can help get you moving, there can be a problem with the timelines we create.

While we discussed this in the Action step, it bears touching on again. There is a germination process to your actions, a time of planting a seed, nurturing it, and watching it grow. Too often, I've seen people abandon a course of action in the Evaluation step because they think things aren't growing fast enough. Too often, we set timelines that don't truly honor the time it takes for something to blossom.

First things first: Have you given your actions some time? Really?

I get wanting to experience fruit from all the effort you've been putting in sooner rather than later. I'm all about finding the quickest routes across town, microwaving things where I can, getting efficient in my actions to hopefully yield a quicker crop. But I find it's most common to expect significant outcomes too early in the game.

Let this soak for a minute:

Time is your friend, friend.

Sure, we've all got someone in our lives who had some kind of viral moment in which it feels like they snapped their fingers, were at the right place at the right time, and went to contract in a millisecond. But those one-offs shouldn't set the standard for how quickly you expect to see the payoffs.

I do understand the concern that someone could put all kinds of time and effort into an endeavor and not appropriately assess if they're

FROM DRIFT TO DRIVE

getting any fruit from it. And, sure, on occasion, I encounter someone who has been doing the same thing over and over and the only result they've really harvested is a big basket of practically nothing.

But when you're following the Seven Step Framework, that won't be a concern for you. Because you will intentionally and systematically take an action and then evaluate the result through the four questions of the Evaluation step, you'll be primed for a clear and honest assessment.

Don't cling to your strategy.

Imagine if your goal was to create the ultimate cookie recipe. You absorbed great info, joined a baking class, worked with a mentor, combined your ingredients, and baked the first batch. You asked yourself the four Evaluation step questions, documenting what you mixed together, how you did it, what you learned about cold versus room temperature butter, and what parts of the baking you enjoyed. As a result, you recognized that what you would do differently next time would be to lower the oven temperature by fifteen degrees and bake the cookies for one minute longer than your first effort.

And then imagine you didn't apply any of that, just headed right back in the kitchen and did the same thing all over again, making no adjustments from what you gleaned in the evaluation of your initial results.

Sounds wild, but I've certainly coached people through the years who have done just that. They hold a proverbial debrief, create a PowerPoint presentation about what would improve the process... and then do nothing in practicum to actually adjust the initial strategy.

STEP 7: EVALUATING

Do you have one of those robotic vacuums at your house? It's a pretty snazzy piece of technology, a little disc on wheels that moves along your floors and sucks up the crumbs and cat hair and general dust of everyday life. The versions on the market today have gotten a lot more sophisticated, but when the appliance first came out two decades ago, it sometimes was a study in going nowhere, in spinning its wheels. The robot vac would encounter a wall or an object in its path and try, again and again, to keep going. It would run into the wall, back up, and run into it again.

Now, admittedly, I'm the guy who in the last chapter preached the power of repetition, and I'll keep talking about it. There's incredible momentum created when you keep your head down and move through the steps, over and over, without allowing yourself to get distracted.

But when we are in this phase of Evaluation, I don't want you to become like that early model of a robotic vacuum, running into the same issue again and again, unable to take an honest assessment or fudging your results under a mask of valuable repetition.

It's not enough to identify what adjustments you should make to your first round of actions; now you need to actually make them. Adjusting your strategy isn't just about philosophically chatting about what might work better; it's actually *doing* those things as you continue to progress forward.

Don't avoid taking responsibility.

We live in a deflection culture. What do I mean by that? Maybe it has something to do with people struggling with self-confidence and pushing away anything that shakes their confidence. Maybe it's

FROM DRIFT TO DRIVE

our highly litigious culture, where people worry about the reputational and financial ramifications if they get blamed for an outcome. Whatever the reason, we often push away our part in the outcomes we create if those outcomes aren't what we wanted, and we love to take full credit for outcomes that speak achievement.

And so, refusing to accept responsibility is something of an epidemic. There's always a reason out there for why someone isn't achieving what they set out to do. There's always something that got in the way or someone who blocked the path.

When it comes to excuses, I've likely heard them all.

My internet went down.

My dog threw up.

It's the political climate.

It's the business climate.

My assistant screwed up.

People don't get it.

People are dumb.

Nobody will give me a break.

And so on and so forth all the way back to "justified" complacency.

Not taking responsibility, making excuses, blaming external factors—it's all part of how we justify complacency in our lives and allow our dreams to go adrift.

As I thought about the development of this chapter and the problem of shirking responsibility and how it sidelines the best of intentions, a part of me wanted to show you some "compassion" and soft-shoe the topic. After all, I'm not here to judge anyone or to come off as uncaring.

STEP 7: EVALUATING

But the more I thought about it, the more important it became to me to simply shoot straight with you, precisely because I *do* care so much and because I *am* a compassionate person. One of the most caring and compassionate things you can do for a person is to tell them the truth, particularly when you see something that is taking them away from the life they desire.

There's a proverb in the Bible that says, "Faithful are the wounds of a friend; but the kisses of an enemy are deceitful" (Proverbs 27:6 KJV). What this conveys to me is that someone who cares will lovingly call you out when needed. So here we go.

Because we live in a culture that deflects responsibility, that seems to only have an appetite for what is seen as "encouragement," we can be blind to the places where we need to own our results. Add to that the tendency to confuse our worth and our identity with our results, and you've got a potion for foggy conditions in your path.

What does it mean to take responsibility for your actions? It means that, when you get a result from your actions, you tell yourself the truth about the relationship between your action and your result.

How do you feel about the caliber of the effort you put into the action?

What can you improve?

I love a quote I saw on Luis Garcia's Instagram feed, (@lawofambition). He posted, "Don't complain about the results you didn't get from the effort you didn't give."[59]

Boom.

Now, this isn't the time to beat yourself up. This isn't the time to look for a place to point the finger of blame. Be a good friend to yourself. Tell yourself the truth about your efforts. Encourage

FROM DRIFT TO DRIVE

yourself to own what outcomes you're achieving. Help you help you, with honesty and honor.

That's the way forward.

Evaluation Reminders

There are two final dangers that you may encounter as you drive through the step of Evaluation. I want to put up yellow caution signs to warn you about these potential road hazards.

Remember, a Result ≠ You

You may be tempted to get your results tangled up in the way you see *yourself*.

Here's a critical reminder: You are not your result.

When you and I care about our dreams, when we invest time and heart and sweat into them, we can sometimes take the result of all that effort on as our identity.

Part of the danger in taking on results as part of our identity is that it can make it really difficult to see clearly what's working and what isn't. When we're honest with ourselves about the results, we get to replicate what's effective and we get to adapt what isn't. That two-step dance keeps us moving across the floor with the momentum we've been building.

When we can't bear to look at the results of our actions because we think it would cost us too much in confidence, in embarrassment, in the way we want to see ourselves? That's a danger zone, friend.

There's another side of the equation as well. Let's say you've gotten a tremendous result from the actions you've taken. You're proud of what you've accomplished, and you should be. However,

STEP 7: EVALUATING

that successful result is also not *you*. Whether a result makes you feel fantastic about yourself or leaves you filled with self-doubt, it's all dangerous territory.

What I sometimes see with people who are getting great results is that they stop learning. They stop evaluating their results honestly. And they stop allowing people to speak into their lives with important feedback. That's a quick way to get yourself thinking that you know it all, you have all the answers, and that your results prove that you're smart and successful.

And it's a house of cards that will tumble the next time you have an unexpected result.

If you're on the opposite side of the coin, feeling terrible about yourself because of a result that feels like a failure, it's all part of the same package. Anytime we allow our results and our identity to get swirled together, we lose sight of the actual road conditions. Overconfidence and under-confidence are the same kind of icy conditions. We hit a patch of reality at some point and we spin out.

I'd love for you to think about your relationship to the Action and Evaluation steps as a lab experiment. A scientist gets curious, let's say, about what would happen if they took an action on a particular chemical. They read the literature and existing research, converse with their colleagues, and set up the experiment. They conduct the experiment and record the results. They then adjust for the next experiment based on the evaluation of how the initial experiment went.

Now, imagine if that scientist had hinged her personal identity to the outcome of the experiment. Imagine if she lost her confidence in preparing for the next experiment. You and I, standing outside the

FROM DRIFT TO DRIVE

laboratory door, would easily be able to see the difference between the scientist as a person and the outcomes of the experiment she was conducting.

That's how I want you to see the action you take and the result you receive. It's a lab, if you will, a place where you're trying things out. You're replicating what worked and you're adjusting to what could be more effective and efficient. And the experiment is not you. You are you; the experiment is the experiment.

Never Confuse Evaluation with Action

You've been pushing hard, learning new things, doing new things, leaving complacency in the dust.

One yellow warning sign remains: Evaluation is not the destination.

A friend of mine was on a long road trip with his family. They'd piled their kids in the family SUV, driven over twelve hundred miles to make some memories up in the mountains for a few days, then turned the SUV around and started the twelve-hundred-mile drive home.

I don't know if you've made a long road trip with a bunch of small kids, but I can assure you it involves lots of potty breaks, chocolate milk spilled in the floorboards, small border wars breaking out over seat allotments, and trying to catch catnaps in the middle of this chaos so you're ready for your turn at the wheel. My friend's road trip was hitting all the notes when it comes to many miles on the road with many tiny children.

In the middle of the night, at about hour twenty-two on their return trip, the steering wheel started to pull a bit to the left. It was

STEP 7: EVALUATING

time for yet another fuel stop and potty break anyway, so my friend pulled over at the closest gas station. They were still a couple of hours from home, and the fatigue of being on the road that long had set in. So when that quick pit stop revealed that a tire was losing air, that news wasn't met with the most excited of attitudes.

From what I understand, there was some caffeine and some Fix-A-Flat and some, um, colorful words that flew over the next little while, as my friend and his wife tried to determine what to do about the tire.

Now, imagine if at this point in the road trip, the couple took a look at the tire, evaluated its degree of flatness, congratulated themselves on diagnosing the issue, and then...just stopped. They wouldn't have made it to their destination—home, sweet home.

I've seen this happen with people. Because Evaluation is the last step, people mistake it for the city limit sign, instead of a mileage sign. Or, because they are good at finding problems, they decide to set up permanent camp in the land of Evaluation, dismantling their Action efforts by identifying what went wrong, but never moving forward on ideas and redos to make things right.

Evaluation, done correctly, will lead you back to Action. The next action will then lead you to Evaluation. This is the process that keeps your tires moving forward, eating up the miles, keeping you on the road. All those actions added up, all those honest and productive evaluations in total, are leading you where you want to go, one rotation at a time.

SECTION THREE:

BACK
IN THE
DRIVER'S
SEAT

When Reality Meets the Road

H ave you heard of Charles D. Scanlon?
I hadn't either until I started the research for this book. But I can promise you, if you've ever spent time on roadways and highways, you've seen his work.

He's the guy you can thank when you avoid the pothole, stay out of the fresh tar, and safely navigate a lane closure. Back in the 1940s, Charles came up with the traffic cone, that twenty-eight-inch, tall, rubbery orange pyramid that keeps you in your lane even when the road conditions are dangerous. He made his first version from old tires and added a grayish-white coat of paint. The next several iterations became more streamlined and standardized, and orange ultimately became the signature color we all recognize at a glance today.[60]

FROM DRIFT TO DRIVE

Now, it would be understandable if you assumed that Charles Scanlon came up with the traffic cone because of having a career in road safety or traffic management, like the folks we talked about in the first chapter who developed rumble strips for highways during the same era. However, Charles created the traffic cone from a different perspective of experience. He was a road painter, and he got tired of people driving over the fresh stripes he'd just painted on the asphalt. So to make his job a little easier, he came up with the traffic cone. The idea was so effective, and people understood that triangle in the middle of the road so well, that the traffic cone found itself as the bright orange mascot for any number of road issues.

Rumble strips and traffic cones—solutions to different problems: one to keep you from distraction and drifting, one to keep you from driving where you shouldn't. That's what I've wanted to be for you on this journey we've made together, and it's the overall goal for the Seven Step Framework.

The finish line is in sight, but there are just a couple of rumble strips and traffic cones left for the Seven Step Framework to do for you.

Hustle Who?

You've encountered a lot of my favorite words throughout these pages. *Drive. Momentum. Speed. Passion. Vision. Excellence. Forward.*

One word you haven't seen promoted here is *hustle.*

"Hustle Culture" has been the "it" girl in entrepreneurship and personal development for the last twenty years or so. It's a quick solution thrown at any roadblock or excuse when someone isn't hitting their targets:

WHEN REALITY MEETS THE ROAD

He just needs to hustle more.

Put some hustle muscle into it.

Every day I'm hustling.

Get up and grind.

Hustle culture is often defined as "a push to work harder to get ahead by any means necessary, often at the expense of self-care and the employee's mental and physical health. In hustle culture, overworking is glamorized and seen as a badge of honor."[61]

If you think the solution to complacency is hustle, then I'm throwing a traffic cone right here in the middle of the road. Hustle is not necessary *and* it's dangerous.

You now have the Seven Step Framework, which gives you what you need to create an efficient, purposeful drive forward. Thinking that hustle—more hours, more frantic and random activity, more spinning, more spreadsheets—is somehow going to get you where you're going is like thinking you can safely drive on ice.

If you're using the Seven Step Framework as an excuse to be sloppy with your time, to justify unbalanced workaholism, or to keep your relationships and other priorities secondary to your hustle, you'll quickly be all the way back to Camp Complacency, not Your Best Next-Chapter Acres.

Why?

Because you'll just be fooling yourself.

That's one of the funny things about the word *hustle*. It isn't only a noun that means hurried, frantic activity. It's also a verb that means to fool someone, to hustle them out of their money through a shady game.

When you hustle, you hustle yourself.

FROM DRIFT TO DRIVE

The Seven Step Framework is targeted. Specific. Measured and thoughtful. Moving from complacency isn't about more, more, more. It's about doing what is *most* important to you, what is *most* fulfilling, what is *most* aligned with being your best. It's not about doing all the things; it's about doing the things that are your all.

We see it at the gym. Someone rolls in, gabbing into their headphones on a work call, huge workout bag on their shoulder, juggling keys and jacket and water bottle and protein bar in their hands. They dump all their cargo in front of a weight machine, still talking loudly at whoever is on the other end of the phone. They jump on the weight machine and start yanking the bar up to their chin, as fast as they can, as many times as they can, however they can.

Now, were you to bring a fitness expert in to watch this performance, they'd have some things to say. Sure, the fitness expert would likely give this chaotic gym-goer some points for at least showing up and getting to the weight machine. But their discerning eye would also look at this hustle form of workout and see the gaps.

The most efficient and effective way to build muscle and make gains is in the form. In the way the weight is lifted and lowered. The jerky, "whatever it takes" speed round our chaotic gym-goer uses will ultimately leave him at greater risk for injury and at a slower speed for gains. One day he finally might get some bulk on him, but he won't have the sculpted biceps and triceps he's looking for. And check this out: Research shows that doing one set with proper form is more effective in building muscle than doing three to four sets with poor form.[62] That means our chaotic gym-goer is spending triple or quadruple the time and effort but getting poorer results.

Look, you know I'm passionate about you busting through the

WHEN REALITY MEETS THE ROAD

complacency that drags you back. But I want to make sure there's a clear traffic cone as you drive forward so you won't confuse the Seven Step Framework with hustle and end up down the wrong ramp. Effort, heart, discipline, and hard work? Sure, those are elemental components of how you apply the Seven Step Framework in your life. But hustling will just have you grinding gears and being busy for busy's sake. You've got far better things to accomplish in your life than busywork.

Working Out

You would think that my wife has already accomplished plenty. She's an amazing mom to triplets, twins, and our singleton. She keeps the wheels rolling on our family life, somehow keeps all the Robinson people heading to all the activities with all the needed equipment and accessories. She is my trusted business partner, friend, and love.

But Jenee still takes it up a notch.

She's also into CrossFit and training and nutrition. She works those abs and puts in the time and eats the broccoli. The girl gets results and she looks and feels fantastic.

I admire those abs. I really do. I want some for myself.

There's just one problem.

It's licorice.

Well, technically, it's not even actually licorice. That's because it's red licorice, which has no real licorice in it. I love the stuff. *Hey, Chris! What's your favorite lunch?* Twizzlers. *What's your favorite snack?* Twizzlers. *What's your favorite pick-me-up?* Twizzlers.

You get it. Twizzlers is pretty much the answer to any favorite-food question for me.

197

FROM DRIFT TO DRIVE

Why Twizzlers over Red Vines? Because I only want the best. Fight me.

So, yes, I'd love to have some well-defined abs. It's just that I want my Twizzlers too. And I'm not real big on having to do the kind of workouts Jenee does to achieve what she does. I'm happy to chase a ball across a pickleball court, and it certainly keeps me in decent shape. But taking it up a notch to pushing tractor tires across hot pavement at five in the humid-Florida morning and doing sit-ups by the dozens as the sun just starts to rise?

Thanks, but I'll be over here watching, snacking on a Twizzlers.

I'm just being a truth-teller about abs and red licorice and me.

And that's what the Seven Step Framework is as well, a truth-teller.

What do I mean by that?

You now know how to make your first round of the Seven Step Framework. I hope by this point you've jumped into working through each of the steps. And where you've arrived to date is at the intersection of Truth and Reality.

As you're moving through the steps, I think it's very likely that you've found new motivation, that you're waking up looking forward to the day, excited to fulfill your index card questions, learning a little and doing a little and evaluating those results. I'm excited for you and I'm excited to see what's next.

But what if that motivation hasn't shown up for you?

In that case, you've likely hitched a ride on a vision that isn't really yours; it doesn't make your heart pump a little faster, and it isn't your honest heading.

It's like abs and Twizzlers and me. I can tell you with great clarity how great it would be to have abs and I can tell you with great

WHEN REALITY MEETS THE ROAD

clarity how to get there. It's just that, truth be told, I'm not willing to do what it takes.

Back at the first step, back when you developed clarity about what you said you wanted, you embarked on a journey. You said you wanted to achieve a certain goal, to come to a particular result. Having gone through the Seven Step Framework, you now have a realistic taste of what it takes to ultimately reach that goal. So here's the question: Are you willing to do it, to make the next several rounds of the Framework? Are you willing to pay the price, show up, improve each time around the track?

That's the Truth part. This is the moment you need to be honest with yourself.

As you reflect on this first round of the Seven Step Framework, take a moment here at the intersection of Truth and Reality. How do you feel?

Are you feeling a little hesitant? A little tired or apathetic? Pulled in a couple of different directions or a little frantic?

Or...

Are you excited? Do you feel the juice to take the next step, and the next? Are you curious about how the coming days will play out? Are you ready to learn more, do more, and evaluate the results?

Whichever way you feel, it's time to begin your second round of the Seven Step Framework.

First, head back to the CAP, the Complacency Assessment Profile, in the second chapter, take it again, and see what progress you're making in your overall relationship to complacency. Then dive back into working through the seven steps now that you've got one round under your belt.

FROM DRIFT TO DRIVE

When I say you've made your first round of the Seven Step Framework, I'm not playing around by calling it the first round. What, you thought you'd move through the seven steps and be done? What kind of friend would I be if I let you get away with that?

Just as the Action and Evaluation steps run on a loop together, you will reach a point when you need to go back to the beginning and run through *all* the steps. Yes, all seven steps run on a loop. Whatever your Evaluation experience has yielded, however you feel in this moment, this intersection of Truth and Reality leads you back to the first lap, back to Clarity. You've either gained even more clarity about your excitement for your vision or you've gained a different kind of clarity that shows you there is still work to be done on creating a *next* for yourself that captures your imagination and revs your engine.

Either way, you've taken an action, and you've gotten a result, not just toward the goal you originally set out, but also toward better understanding yourself and what you want. You need to take that new clarity and gather new resources, filter through them, possibly seek new guides and relationships or seek different answers from those you have, and let all of that direct you to new actions, which you will in turn evaluate.

Now is the time to begin again.

That's cutting the head off the complacency monster, one round at a time.

It Was There All the Time

When I was a kid growing up in Oklahoma, I don't think it ever would have occurred to me that I would be traveling the world, speaking to amazing people, helping others achieve their dreams.

WHEN REALITY MEETS THE ROAD

And yet now, with a passport full of stamps, I gratefully find that that's my life.

One of my favorite parts of the travel I do is the people I get to meet along the way. Sometimes it's a guy in Indonesia who hates being a lawyer and who also appreciates a great jazz combo, like the new friend I told you about meeting in the Relationships step.

Sometimes it's the fascinating guy who keeps all the flower beds at a hotel blossoming and blooming beyond anything I've ever seen, and he's got incredible stories about his life to share. Sometimes it's the people in high positions and sometimes it's the people who help make the conference rooms clean and welcoming and who bring in the delicious food.

On a recent trip to Cambodia, the same trip I shared with you in the second chapter where my fascination with the problem of complacency first ignited, I got to meet with that nation's minister of education. While you might think that he would share with me all kinds of insight about teachers and students and classrooms, he was also someone who told me something about his life experience that has really stuck with me.

He told me about his house. "My home is on a rice farm. I get to watch the process of the rice growing and being harvested, how the crop is grown in fields that look like ponds because of the water level needed for growing rice." He talked about the incredible green color of the rice as it grows.

And then he told me about something I'd never heard before.

At the end of the rice harvest, they burn the rice field. The water is drained and the whole patch is set on fire. What had been this beautiful shade of bright green is now a field of ashes. It's dark.

FROM DRIFT TO DRIVE

It's ugly. It doesn't look like there's any life left in it.

But, he said, when the first rain comes after the field has been burned, practically overnight the field turns green again.

"It shows me," he explained, "that even when something looks like it has no life left to it, even when the view from where I'm sitting looks terrible, no matter how things look, with just a drop of rain, there is life there, waiting to be lived out."

It really hit me that that's what our time in this book has been about. Your next chapter of your beautiful life, the pages in which you'll find even greater expression of the wisdom you've gained and the experiences you've had and the heart you have to share, it's been there the whole time. There are fields of possibility in your life, dreams you thought didn't have any pulse left in them. But the Seven Step Framework is a way to put some raindrops into the mix, to begin stirring new life. As things green up, there will be further work to do, more information to gather, more guidance to receive. But let this first round of engaging the Seven Step Framework show you the life that is right there, no matter what it looks like at the moment.

In the end, assuming a field is done is complacency, right? Not making the effort to share a few sprinkles of attention, not wondering what might be there. Accepting that a burned-out field is simply that—a harvest of ash. Maybe you've settled, accepted that a path you dreamed of exploring doesn't hold promise. Maybe you've become okay with your life not looking the way you thought it would.

But what about trying a little water? A little nurturing?

Complacency, particularly when you've experienced previous

WHEN REALITY MEETS THE ROAD

success, is something you conquer over and over again. And no matter your age or stage of life, there are still the seeds of dreams living right beneath the grit.

Have you ever met someone who seemed...old? Now that I'm in my mid-forties, I'm surprised by a number of my peers who are suddenly talking about themselves as if they've lived nine or ten decades. "My hip is driving me crazy. I guess that's what getting old will do to you." "I keep forgetting where I put my keys. Just my old brain." "I can't wear an outfit like that. I'm too old." They keep declaring complacency over their lives, even though there are plenty of birthdays left to go.

Here's the thing: I know eighty-year-olds who are excited and energized by life. They are learning, working, trying new things. And I know thirty-year-olds who've had a little success and a little experience who have allowed complacency to move into the house, a messy, lazy roommate they don't have the guts to kick out. Marv Levy, the legendary Buffalo Bills coach who, as of this writing, is ninety-nine years old, said, "Experience should be a plus as long as it doesn't become complacency. If you say, 'We're not going to change; we didn't do it that way before,' then you've become too old."[63]

I'm on a mission to one day be the youngest ninety-nine-year-old you'll ever meet, a millionaire of stories and mission and vision. Which means I'm going to fight off the complacency that would attempt to keep me from my goal.

*   *   *

I had someone reach out to me who wanted to talk about finances. They'd observed my business and financial success through the years

FROM DRIFT TO DRIVE

and wanted some advice about how I look at investments and planning. Their path to having money was unique. They had unexpectedly come into a large sum.

When I got on the phone with them, they were excited to tell me about the financial windfall they'd received. They were brimming with questions and ideas as I listened to their nervous and elated chatter.

"So what do you think?" they exclaimed.

I responded with this:

"Congratulations on becoming a millionaire. Now you're going to have to learn to be one."

We've got a million ideas and directions we can go, you and I. We just need to learn how to *be* one of them. And then we can learn how to be the next one. And the next. That's how I see your ongoing journey: continuing to win the battle against complacency, continuing to grow and build and thrive. All the way up to a million realized actions and results that fill out the next stories in our lives. That's a life well lived and a story worth telling.

I didn't know when starting this book how challenging it would be to end it. I think it's because this is the part of the road trip with you where I have you drop me off and continue on your way.

Are you going to follow the directions I've written out for you?

Are you awake enough to be on the road? Without me constantly talking in your ear, are you going to keep your eyes on the road, all the way to where you say you want to go?

I know you've got this. Yes, you may have some adjustments to make, now that we've completed this first lap around the track. But I know that each time you make a pit stop at the Clarity step, you'll

WHEN REALITY MEETS THE ROAD

double-check you're clear on where you're going. When you get your maps at the Gathering and Filtering steps, you'll find even better routes to take. When you have Guidance and Relationships hop in for the ride, you'll have even better support and community to go with you. And with each turn you take in Action, and in each result you observe in Evaluation, you'll get better and better at being right in the center of *your* lane.

You've got this, friend.

What do you want?

Well, go get it.

Do something today to get there.

And I'll wave to you from my lane.

Godspeed, friend. Godspeed.

ACKNOWLEDGMENTS

I would like to express my heartfelt gratitude to all those who have supported me throughout the journey of writing this book.

First and foremost, I am deeply grateful to my wife, Jenee, whose unwavering support and encouragement have been a constant source of inspiration. Without your belief in me, this book would not have been possible.

Lorna Weston-Smyth, I am grateful for your tireless work and support to help me serve and live out my dream of adding value to people on a daily basis.

To my parents, I.C. and Pat Robinson, thank you for your patience, understanding, and love. Your sacrifices and words of encouragement have been invaluable throughout my life.

I would also like to extend my appreciation to Julie Lyles Carr, whose expertise, feedback, and attention to detail helped shape this book into its final form.

This book contains stories of so many who have guided, supported, and mentored me throughout my life, and I would not be

ACKNOWLEDGMENTS

who I am today without them. They include David Blunt, John C. Maxwell, Lethia Owens, Mark Cole, Jason Jacobs, Roddy Galbraith, Scott Fay, Paul Martinelli, Kelly Dellasalla, and Craig Ratliff.

To my Maxwell Leadership Team—Chris Goede, Jared Cagle, George Hoskins, John Griffin, Chad Johnson, Reggie Goodin, Greg Steely—thank you for everything you do daily to add value to people around the world.

Finally, I am grateful to all the readers, whether near or far, for embracing this content and for sharing in the journey.

Thank you all for your kindness, support, and faith in this work.

NOTES

1. Edward J. Watts, "Complacency—Not Hubris—Is What Killed the Roman Republic," *Zocalo Public Square*, February 26, 2019, https://www.zocalopublicsquare.org/2019/02/26/complacency-not-hubris-killed-roman-republic/ideas/essay/.

2. SI Staff, "The King," *Sports Illustrated*, October 19, 1992, https://vault.si.com/vault/1992/10/19/the-king-richard-petty-is-closing-his-remarkable-35-year-reign-over-stock-car-racing-with-a-regal-tour.

3. Bill Gates with Nathan Myhrvold and Peter Rinearson, *The Road Ahead* (Viking, 1995).

4. Mark Loproto, "What Is Victory Disease?" PearlHarbor.org, August 22, 2019, https://pearlharbor.org/blog/what-is-victory-disease/.

5. "Battle of Midway," *Encyclopaedia Britannica*, last modified February 10, 2025, https://www.britannica.com/event/Battle-of-Midway.

6. Loproto, "What Is Victory Disease?"

7. "Strong's H7962 – Shaqat," *Blue Letter Bible*, accessed February 11, 2025, https://www.blueletterbible.org/lexicon/h7962/kjv/wlc/0-1/.

8. "Termites 101: A South Florida Homeowner's Guide," *Hulett Environmental Services Blog*, accessed February 11, 2025, https://www.bugs.com/blog/termites-101-a-south-florida-homeowners-guide/.

9. Liz Willding Robbins, "The Real Cost of Complacency: How to Reduce Burnout," *Insigniam*, October 3, 2022, https://insigniam.com/how-to-reduce-burnout-from-complacency/.

NOTES

10. Christy Bieber, "Leading Causes of Divorce: 43% Report Lack of Family Support," *Forbes Advisor*, last updated October 18. 2024, https://www.forbes.com/advisor/legal/divorce/common-causes-divorce/.

11. Benjamin E. Mays Historic Site (@benjaminemays), "The tragedy of life is often not in our failure…," Facebook, May 24, 2019, https://www.facebook.com/share/p/15V5XZzCew/.

12. "Rumble Strip," *Wikipedia: The Free Encyclopedia*, accessed February 11, 2025, https://en.wikipedia.org/wiki/Rumble_strip.

13. Federal Highway Administration, "Chapter 2: Safety Effectiveness of Center Line and Shoulder Rumble Strips," *FHWA Safety*, accessed February 11, 2025, https://safety.fhwa.dot.gov/roadway_dept/pavement/rumble_strips/fhwasa16115/ch2.cfm.

14. Lennox Lewis (@lennoxlewis), "Sometimes success needs interruption to regain focus and shake off complacency," X, February 15, 2012, https://x.com/LennoxLewis/status/169880482086006784.

15. J. C. Grew, *Turbulent Era: A Diplomatic Record of Forty Years 1904-1945* (Houghton Mifflin, 1952).

16. Dean LeBaron, Romesh Vaitilingam and Marilyn Pitchford, *The Ultimate Book of Investment Quotations* (Capstone, 1999), ePDF, https://epdf.pub/the-ultimate-book-of-investment-quotations.html.

17. image: Flaticon.com.

18. Scott Miker, "Content not Complacent," ScottMiker.com, accessed April 28, 2025, https://www.scottmiker.com/content-not-complacent.

19. Drew Brees, *Coming Back Stronger: Unleashing the Hidden Power of Adversity* (Tyndale House Publishers, 2010), 80.

20. "Chevrolet Camaro," Wikipedia: The Free Encyclopedia, accessed February 11, 2025, https://en.wikipedia.org/wiki/Chevrolet_Camaro.

21. Joseph Allen, "The No.1 Eye Doctor: They're Lying To You About Blue Light! The Truth About Floaters!" posted October 3, 2024, by The Diary of A CEO, YouTube, 13:17, https://www.youtube.com/watch?v=SWjzjClBCO4.

22. Dr. Joseph Allen, *The No.1 Eye Doctor: They're Lying To You About Blue Light! The Truth About Floaters!*, interviewed by Steven Bartlett, *The Diary of a CEO*, podcast, April 22, 2024, https://podcasts.apple.com/us/podcast/the-no-1-eye-doctor-theyre-lying-to-you-about-blue/id1291423644?i=1000671633896.

23. National Geographic. "Sir Edmund Hillary and Tenzing Norgay Summited Mount Everest in 1953," *National Geographic*, accessed March 24, 2025, https://www.nationalgeographic.com/adventure/article/sir-edmund-hillary-tenzing-norgay-1953.

NOTES

24. Himalayan Trust, "Himalayan Trust," accessed March 24, 2025, https://himalayan-trust.org/.

25. *Encyclopaedia Britannica*, s.v. "Hydra," accessed March 24, 2025, https://www.britannica.com/topic/Hydra-Greek-mythology.

26. Spencer McKee, "Two of World's Most Dangerous Airports Located in Colorado," *The Denver Gazette*, March 13, 2023, https://denvergazette.com/outtherecolorado/news/two-of-worlds-most-dangerous-airports-located-in-colorado/article_b082c920-7eae-58d6-85fe-5a35d8e8c946.html.

27. Albert Bigelow Paine, *Mark Twain: A Biography: The Personal and Literary Life of Samuel Langhorne Clemens*, Vol. 3 (Harper & Brothers, 1912), "Chapter 251: A Lobbying Expedition," 1343.

28. TRUTHPLANE, https://truthplane.com/.

29. Stephen Shapiro, "Stop Worrying About the Novelty of Your Ideas," *Inc.*, August 22, 2020, https://www.inc.com/stephen-shapiro/stop-worrying-about-novelty-of-your-ideas.html.

30. Y.H. Chang, I.C. Wu, and C.A. Hsiung, "Reading Activity Prevents Long-Term Decline in Cognitive Function in Older People: Evidence from a 14-year Longitudinal Study," *International Psychogeriatrics* 33, no. 1 (January 2021): 63-74, https://doi.org/10.1017/S1041610220000812.

31. David Nield, "People Who Read Books Live Almost 2 Years Longer, Study Finds," *ScienceAlert*, August 10, 2016, https://www.sciencealert.com/spending-more-time-reading-could-help-you-live-longer-suggests-a-new-study.

32. "Reading Reduces Stress. Fact.," *Newcastle University Medical Literature*, blog, January 19, 2023, https://blogs.ncl.ac.uk/medlit/2023/01/19/reading-reduces-stress-fact/.

33. Nick Politan, "Science Says If You Read Books You'll Earn More Money," *Electric Literature*, June 10, 2016, https://electricliterature.com/science-says-if-you-read-books-youll-earn-more-money/.

34. "Adults Spend Staggering Number of Hours Watching TV Every Week," *Movieguide*, January 5, 2024, https://www.movieguide.org/news-articles/adults-spend-staggering-number-of-hours-watching-tv-weekly.html.

35. Blinkist, https://www.blinkist.com/.

36. Infinite Mind, https://infinitemind.io/.

37. Evelyn Wood Speed Reading & Memory Training, Pryor Learning, https://www.pryor.com/training-categories/evelyn-wood-speed-reading-resources/.

38. Paul Scheele, "Your Next Level with Photo Reading," posted October 13, 2001, by Learning Strategies, YouTube, 1:01:07, https://www.youtube.com/watch?v=hKWC6hn7x8w.

NOTES

39. Douglas Heingartner, "Now Hear This, Quickly," *The New York Times*, October 2, 2003, https://www.nytimes.com/2003/10/02/technology/now-hear-this-quickly.html.

40. "Barriers to Effective Listening," *Can't We All Just Get Along?*, University of West Florida Pressbooks, accessed May 12, 2025, https://pressbooks.uwf.edu/cantwejustgetalong /chapter/barriers-to-effective-listening/#:~:text=Difference%20between%20speech %20and%20thought,minute%20(Hargie%2C%202011).

41. Stephen Pierce, "Mind Mapping by Stephen Pierce," posted June 7, 2006, by @impuls-siveprofits, YouTube, 7:42, https://www.youtube.com/watch?v=uvnbKEHOQIY.

42. Madhanraj Kalyanasundaram et al., "Effectiveness of Mind Mapping Technique in Information Retrieval Among Medical College Students in Puducherry—A Pilot Study," *Indian Journal of Community Medicine* 42, no. 1 (January 2017): 19–23, https://doi.org/10.4103/0970-0218.199793.

43. Raphaela Brandner, "Why Mind Mapping? 5 Key Benefits (+ Templates)," *MeisterTask,* blog, February 15, 2024, https://www.meistertask.com/blog/why-mind-mapping.

44. iThoughts on iPad, toketaWare, https://www.toketaware.com/ithoughts-ios.

45. Reuters, "Nepali Sherpa Scales Everest for Record 30th Time," CNN, May 22, 2024, https://www.cnn.com/2024/05/22/travel/kami-rita-sherpa-nepal-everest-record-intl -scli/index.html.

46. Grace Winstanely, "Mentoring Statistics You Need to Know—2024," *Mentorloop,* blog, February 21, 2024, https://mentorloop.com/blog/mentoring-statistics/.

47. *Online Etymology Dictionary*, s.v. "proximity," https://www.etymonline.com /search?q=proximity.

48. Angela Benavides, "Everest 2023 Final Death Toll: The Deadliest Season Ever," *ExplorersWeb*, December 11, 2023, https://explorersweb.com/everest-final-2023 -death-toll-worst-ever/.

49. Alan Arnette, "How Much Does It Cost to Climb Mount Everest?—2025 Edition," *Alan Arnette* (blog), January 13, 2025, https://www.alanarnette.com/blog/2025/01/13 /how-much-does-it-cost-to-climb-everest-2025-edition/.

50. Valorie Burton, https://valorieburton.com/.

51. Nola Taylor Tillman, "Nicolaus Copernicus Biography: Facts & Discoveries," Space.com, January 17, 2022, https://www.space.com/15684-nicolaus -copernicus.html.

52. "Cohort," *Encyclopaedia Britannica*, accessed February 11, 2025, https://www.britannica.com/topic/cohort-Roman-military.

53. Anwesha Barari, "5 Benefits of Cohort-Based Learning in the Workplace," *Emeritus,* (blog), last updated January 8 2025, https://emeritus.org/blog/cohort-based-learning/.

NOTES

54. Martin R. Huecker et al., *Imposter Phenomenon* (StatPearls Publishing, 2023), introduction, https://www.ncbi.nlm.nih.gov/books/NBK585058/.

55. Selene Yeager, "The Scientific Reason Pelotons Go So Freakin' Fast," Bicycling, August 3, 2018, https://www.bicycling.com/news/a22625969/group-ride-cycling-increases-free-speed/.

56. Denise Jacobs, "Breaking the Perfectionism-Procrastination Infinite Loop," *Web Standards Sherpa*, May 20, 2014, https://webstandardssherpa.com/reviews/breaking-the-perfectionism-procrastination-infinite-loop.html#:~:text=Procrastination%20is%20often%20a%20symptom,or%20unworthy%20inside%20of%20them.

57. Marcel Schwantes, "Science Says Only 8 Percent of People Actually Achieve Their Goals. Here Are 7 Things They Do Differently," *Inc.*, June 13, 2018, https://www.inc.com/marcel-schwantes/science-says-only-8-percent-of-people-actually-achieve-their-goals-here-are-7-things-they-do-differently.html.

58. Brandon Mackie, "Pickleball Statistics: The Numbers Behind America's Fastest-Growing Sport," Pickleheads, updated February 19, 2025, https://www.pickleheads.com/blog/pickleball-statistics.

59. Luis Garcia (@lawofambition), "Don't complain about the results you didn't get…," Instagram, November 18, 2024, https://www.instagram.com/p/DCiA45nyq5g/?utm.

60. "Charles Scanlon: Cone, Cones, Coned," MCA Chicago Plaza Project, April 1, 2017, https://mcachicago.org/publications/blog/2017/04/mca-chicago-plaza-project-charles-scanlon-cone-cones-coned.

61. Anna Picagli, "Hustle Culture in the Workplace—Understanding Its Impact & How to Deal With It," *Workhuman*, blog, January 22, 2025, https://www.workhuman.com/blog/hustle-culture/.

62. Mayo Clinic Staff, "Strength Training: Get Stronger, Leaner, Healthier," Mayo Clinic, accessed February 11, 2025, https://www.mayoclinic.org/healthy-lifestyle/fitness/in-depth/strength-training/art-20046670.

63. Tom Pedulla, "Marv Levy Is an 81-Year-Old Who Refuses to Act His Age," *USA Today*, cited in "Bills Retrofitted with Levy in Front Office," August 15, 2006, GoBengals.com, https://forum.go-bengals.com/index.php?/topic/20774-bills-retrofitted-with-levy-in-front-office/.

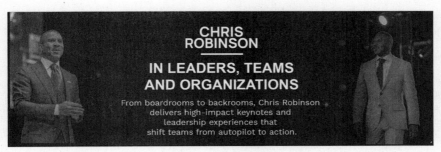

FROM DRIFT TO DRIVE
IS YOUR TEAM DRIFTING OR DRIVING?

Most teams aren't failing – they're drifting. Chris Robinson helps organizations identify hidden complacency, refine clarity and take aligned action using his proven 7-Step Leadership Framework

BOOK CHRIS TO SPEAK

Keynote Experience
High-energy story presentations that transform teams and organizations from the stage.

Corporate Training
Half and full day leadership intensive training that produce measurable results.

SOLUTIONS THAT SPARK MOMENTUM

"One of the most engaging speaker/coaches. One of the most genuine people I have ever listened to. Always engaging."
– Patrick Gonzales, Traffic Manager, Frito Lay

Learn More at
ChrisRobinsonSpeaker.com